"This is exactly the book the world needs now!"

Diana Dentinger
Best-selling author of *Modus Vivendi: Your Life Your Way*

"This book is one of the best business books I have read! This really is a 'must read' for the entrepreneur and small business owner."

Lou Brogan
YOUR LIFE, YOUR MONEY

"Written with wisdom and compassion. Her love for the reader shines through…"

Bernadette Griffiths
NRG REALTY

"Jasmine Sampson brings her solid spiritual credentials to [a] book which is easy to read."

Sarah Deeks
HAMILTON REIKI

Growing Business with Soul

Practical Spirituality for the Busy Entrepreneur

Jasmine Sampson

Copyright © Jasmine Sampson, 2015

www.jasminesampson.com

Transformational Living Publications

National Library of New Zealand:
ISBN: 978-0-473-34213-5
Title: Growing Business With Soul
Author: Jasmine Sampson
Format: Softcover

Publishing Consultant: Linda Diggle, Bookboffin
Internal Layout: Loaded Spring Communication Design
Cover Design: Studio 1 Design

All rights reserved. No part of this publication may be reproduced, stored in a retrieval system, communicated or transmitted in any form or by means, electronic, mechanical, photocopying, recording, or otherwise, without the prior written permission of the author. All inquiries should be made to the publisher.

For Sam, Daniel, Aiden and
the children of the world.

CONTENTS

Preface: How This Book Began ix

Introduction: Maximise Your Impact 1
    This Book Is for You If. 1
    Help for a World in Crisis 2
    The World Doesn't Have to Be This Way! 2
    The How-To of Practical Spirituality 3
    God by Any Other Name … 3
    What You Will Find Inside 4
    Free Online Resources for You 5

Part I: Growing Your Relationship with the Universe 7
Chapter 1: Living in a Conscious Universe 9
    Main Points of This Chapter 15
    What This Means for Your Business 15
    Grow Your Business Action Steps 15
Chapter 2: The Power of Love 16
    Main Points of This Chapter 21
    What This Means for Your Business 21
    Grow Your Business Action Steps 21
    Meditation: Resting in the Heart of Love 22
Chapter 3: Meditate daily 23
    Why Meditate? 23
    Two Major Types of Meditation 26
    Main Points of This Chapter 31
    What This Means for Your Business 32
    Grow Your Business Action Steps 32
Chapter 4: Pray 33
    Main Points of this Chapter 39
    What This Means for Your Business 39
    Grow Your Business Action Steps 39
Chapter 5: Heal Your Trust in the Universe 41
    Main Points of This Chapter 43
    What This Means for Your Business 43
    Grow Your Business Action Steps 43
    Meditation: Healing Your Trust in the Universe 44

Chapter 6: Take Your Place in the Global Jigsaw 47
   Soul Themes 50
   Seven Great Soul Themes 50
   Living Your Soul Theme 51
   Main Points of This Chapter 52
   What This Means for Your Business 52
   Grow Your Business Action Steps 53
   Meditation: Taking Your Place in the Global Jigsaw 53

Chapter 7: Ask for Guidance 57
   Four Principles of Guidance 59
   What This Means for Your Business 61
   Grow Your Business Action Steps 61
   Meditation for Guidance 62

Chapter 8: Harness the Power of Intention 63
   Opening up to Divine Intention 63
   Main Points of This Chapter 68
   What This Means for Your Business 68
   Grow Your Business Action Steps 69
   Meditation: Discovering the Power and Beauty Within 69

Chapter 9: Welcome Your *Shalom* 71
   Main Points of This Chapter 73
   What This Means for Your Business 73
   Grow Your Business Action Steps 73
   Meditation: Getting in Touch with Your Shalom 74

Part II: Growing Your Relationship With Yourself 77

Chapter 10: Embrace Your Uniqueness 79
   Main Points of This Chapter 84
   What This Means for Your Business 85
   Grow Your Business Action Steps 85

Chapter 11: Practise Forgiveness 87
   Healing Processes 91
   A Process to Release Past Pain 92
   Forgiveness Meditation 94
   Main Points of This Chapter 97
   What This Means for Your Business 97
   Grow Your Business Action Steps 97

Part III : Growing Your Relationship with Other People 99
Chapter 12: Let Go of Judgment 101
    Main Points of This Chapter 105
    What This Means for Your Business 105
    Grow Your Business Action Steps 106
    Meditation 106
Chapter 13: Use the Technology of Love 107
    Main Points of This Chapter 110
    What This Means for Your Business 110
    Grow Your Business Action Steps 111
    Loving-Kindness Meditation for Your Business 111

Part IV: Growing Your Relationship with the World Around 113
Chapter 14: Ask for More Money 115
    Main Points of This Chapter 120
    What This Means for Your Business 120
    Grow Your Business Action Steps 120
    Meditation: Opening up to Financial Abundance 121
Chapter 15: Practise Appreciation and Blessing 123
    Appreciation 123
    Blessing 126
    Main Points of This Chapter 130
    What This Means for Your Business 130
    Grow Your Business Action Steps 130
    A Blessing Meditation 131
Chapter 16: An Invitation to the Adventure of Your Lifetime 133
    Stages on the Journey 134

Bibliography 137
Acknowledgments 139

PREFACE
How This Book Began

Just as an acorn comes ready to become an oak tree, provided certain conditions are met, so there is in me, and in you, a potential waiting to be nurtured into being. This book will show you how.

Growing Business with Soul brings together two interwoven strands of my life experience and work.

Thirty years ago I was a young wife and mother, raising three young sons, one of whom had special needs. My husband frequently worked late into the evening and I was battling chronic exhaustion, loneliness, resentment and my own super-high expectations of myself as a wife and mother. I began searching for techniques and strategies to help me cope with life: things to heal the pain within me, and which would do something to help ease the conflict with those around me.

I began the search within my Christian tradition and was blessed to meet with a compassionate and powerful consciousness that was actively involved in helping me release childhood pain and meet the challenges of my daily life. I discovered that I have a gift of healing and the ability to sense the hidden emotions of those on whom I focus my awareness, and I began to use that gift within the context of my church to help others who were struggling as I was. By my late twenties I was passing on to others the techniques I was using myself to cope with life as I experienced it. I do this in different ways now, but the essence of that work remains the same.

The other strand of my life is my sense of being in service to a Higher Power. For as long as I can remember I have been consciously aware of my relationship with the reality and power of the invisible realm we call *spiritual*.

My sense of guidance led me first to teaching, then to focus on my role as a mother and on my own healing. Later came a call to ordination as a Christian minister. I worked for a time as a hospital chaplain, and later as a parish minister, before establishing a spiritual 'drop-in' centre in the heart of our local CBD. Shortly after this I was guided just as clearly to 'follow God into the world' and stepped outside the church to pursue my vocation in the world. Since 2005 I have been entirely outside of organised religion.

In leaving the church I stepped away from a recognised career-and-income path and have had to face the challenges of offering my skills and gifts to the world through the vocation of self-employment. I found that traditional business advice somehow didn't fit me. At some deep level it didn't make sense to me and in trying to apply the strategies I felt like I was trying to force myself into a mould built for somebody else.

I sensed that what I really wanted to do was use the spiritual principles I employ to such good effect in every other part of my life to develop my business, but I didn't have the confidence to do that at first. So I kept on trying to do the traditional thing, working with several different coaches and becoming more and more discouraged and frustrated. The most basic steps eluded me. For example, no matter how much I tried, I just couldn't describe clearly what I was offering or who I was offering it to.

Finally I decided to trust myself and my sense of guidance and let go of trying to be anything other than myself. I recognised that my business wasn't something I needed to *build*. It wasn't something outside of myself and separate from me. Rather, it was something I was *growing*. My call was to allow the business that was *already inside me* to manifest itself into the world.

When I finally stopped turning outwards, decided to trust myself and drew on the personal and spiritual growth tools I had used for years for myself and my clients, I began to make real progress. I let go of all expectations about how my business should be developing and instead concentrated on staying faithful to myself and using the practices and strategies I outline in this book.

Implementing these tools as *deliberate business practices* gave me a sense of peace and progress that had been lacking when I tried to conform to traditional models. I have always loved what I do, but as I persevered I began to experience a whole new level of focus, purpose and fulfilment.

I knew that my business and I were growing, even though I couldn't at first see what the external shape would become.

Using the exact processes I will share with you, I was finally able to lay the solid foundations for business success that I had been unable to do *before I had done the inner work*.

In just six months my business moved from 'barely-getting-by' to thriving:
- I discovered a coach who was offering exactly what I had been looking for.
- I clarified my unique contribution and identified my ideal client group (you!).
- I finished and published this book and developed the online course that accompanies it.
- My income increased ten-fold.
- I moved from only seeing clients 1-1 to having a vibrant online business with an international impact.

My life's passion is to evolve spiritually, mentally and emotionally, and my work has always been to share with others the techniques and practices that help me. This book is a constellation of the best of my life's discoveries. *Growing Business with Soul* gives you the strategies and tools that I have used to grow a thriving business doing what I love and am uniquely gifted to do, and living from the love, peace and joy that is the essence of every human being.

You can do the same.

INTRODUCTION
Maximise Your Impact

As an entrepreneur, you are already demonstrating leadership, courage and creativity. You have the potential to be one of the forerunners of changing human consciousness.

This Book Is for You If…

- You are an entrepreneur with a desire to fulfil the highest possibility for your life
- You want to put your skills and experience at the service of humanity as a whole
- The concept that your business is a potential *inside of you* that you want to grow makes sense to you
- You find that traditional business models don't quite fit you *or*
- They used to work ok but aren't any longer *and/or*
- You sense that more is possible for you but don't quite know how to achieve it

This book is also for you if…

- You consider yourself spiritual, but not religious
- You would like a framework of meaning to support you in life and in business
- You would like a set of simple and effective practices that will empower you to navigate the 'unknown territory' of your future with confidence and joy
- The idea of building your business in partnership with a Higher Consciousness excites you

Help for a World in Crisis

We are living in a time of unprecedented movement and upheaval. Everything is changing, not just at the level of society and economics, but at the deeper level of human consciousness itself.

It is fairly obvious that this planet will not sustain the burden of environmental exploitation that has been placed upon it in recent centuries. The economic models of the industrial age – rampant consumerism and consumption of the Earth's resources without regard for the future – cannot continue. Sickness, poverty, famine and violence continue to be the experience of millions of people all around the world.

Humankind has lived with these problems for centuries, and all our attempts to eradicate them have failed. Technology has enabled us to travel into space and communicate across the world in a matter of seconds, but has failed to address the real problems of the human heart and spirit.

The World Doesn't Have to Be This Way!

The problems we see around us are expressions of deep beliefs we hold about ourselves as a species and as individuals. It is a well-known truth that a problem cannot be solved from the mindset that created it, and attending to society's problems without addressing their underlying cause is a fruitless exercise.

Our personal and collective suffering is rooted in the deep sense of alienation and loneliness that lies in the human heart. We feel isolated: from unacknowledged parts of ourselves, from other people, from nature and from the creative Life Force. Nothing less than a deep healing of the human heart, and a new vision of ourselves and our relationship with the world around us, will be sufficient to overcome the challenges we face.

Healing your heart *and* helping you to fulfil the highest possibility for your life and your business are the dual aims of this book.

If you care about peace, about justice, about poverty and world hunger, about the environment, then you have in your hands the tools needed to make real and lasting change at the place where our troubles all start – at the level of human consciousness itself. The world needs people who are willing to let go of the old models of belief, feeling, thought and action and evolve into new ones.

As an entrepreneur, you are already demonstrating leadership by stepping away from existing structures to forge a path of your own. With this courage and creativity you have the potential to be one of the forerunners of changing human consciousness. The practices and principles in this book will teach you how to partner consciously with the creative energy of the universe to maximise your impact and create even greater levels of fulfilment.

If you are ready to respond to the next evolutionary pressure, move beyond the limits of your ego-mind and embrace your quantum potential, then this book is your 'how-to' manual.

The How-To of Practical Spirituality

This is a book about practical spirituality. In it, I share with you the ideas and practices that have evolved for me over more than 30 years of conscious spiritual development, training and work: first as a teacher and mother, then as hospital chaplain and parish minister, and later as a workshop facilitator, life coach and spiritual mentor.

My 'working spirituality' is primarily shaped by my experience, both inside and outside the Christian Church, in conversation with a wide variety of traditions and teachers, from the ancient spiritual truths spoken about in all of the great religions, through modern spiritual teachers to the discoveries of quantum science.

God by Any Other Name ...

In a book of practical spirituality one must inevitably talk about a Higher Power or Higher Consciousness – *God*.

The word 'God' is a severely limited and negative concept for many people. Although linguistically it comes from the same root as the word 'good,' the cultural associations of medieval theology and the history of Christendom make this a term loaded with negative associations for most people in the Western World. Accordingly, throughout this text I seldom use it.

My concept of God is the underlying, organising Consciousness of the Cosmos – what Gregg Braden refers to as the *Divine Matrix* and Dr. Amit Goswami calls *The Ground of All Being*. I usually refer to this reality as *Life Force*, *Source*, *Spirit*, and *Higher Consciousness*.

When you see these terms, please substitute the word(s) that are most useful to you and your belief system.

What You Will Find Inside

As you will learn in Chapter 1, we live in a universe of interconnected relationships. I have organised this book in four parts, based roughly upon four different areas of relationship we find in our lives. Inevitably there is some overlap of concepts, and the practices of one part can be applied to all.

Part I is the longest section and looks at growing your relationship with the universe itself.

- Chapter 1 explores the concept of a *Conscious Universe*, while Chapter 2 examines the nature and *Power of Love* as the creative power at the heart of the cosmos. Having explored foundational principles, we then move on to practices to help you and your business grow.
- Chapter 3, *Daily Meditation*, and Chapter 4, entitled *Pray*, go hand in hand as they explore two ways to develop an intimate relationship with the Life Force.
- Chapter 5 focuses on our existential fear and provides a meditation to *Heal Your Trust in the Universe*.
- Chapter 6, *Take Your Place in the Global Jigsaw*, discusses your unique contribution to the world and takes a look at Soul Themes.
- Chapter 7 teaches you ways to *Ask for Guidance* and Chapter 8 shows you how to *Harness the Power of Intention*.
- Having put these principles into practice you can now *Welcome Your Shalom,* as described in Chapter 9.

Part II has two chapters focused on growing your relationship with yourself:

- Chapter 10 invites you to *Embrace Your Uniqueness*, and Chapter Eleven looks at how to *Practise Forgiveness*.

Part III presents transformative practices for your relationships with other people:

- Chapter 12 encourages you to *Let Go of Judgement*, while Chapter 13 explains how to *Use the Technology of Love*.

Part IV looks at your relationship with the world around you:

- Chapter 14 shows you how to *Ask for More Money*, while Chapter 15 focuses on *Appreciation and Blessing*.

In each chapter, I provide a theoretical framework to explain a principle or practice, together with examples of how this can be applied in everyday life. Each chapter ends with a summary of main points and a short paragraph explaining what this means for your business, plus suggested *Grow Your Business Action Steps*. In most cases there is also a meditation process for you to use.

Free Online Resources for You

As well as the wealth of meditations, exercises and processes in this text, I have created online a series of resources as a gift to readers of this book. You can watch videos, listen to meditations, explore supplementary material, and download full instructions for all my favourite transformational processes at www.JasmineSampson.com/bookresources

How to Use this Book

Parts of this book will be more interesting and/or useful to you than others. That is the way it should be. I suggest that you read through the book quickly for an overview and then return to work through the exercises and meditations.

Chapter 3, *Meditation*, Chapter 11, *Forgiveness*, and Chapter 15, *Blessing*, are foundational practices. Begin with the exercises in these chapters and then move onto the parts that interest you most. Practise a meditation or exercise until it no longer feels alive for you, then choose another. As you develop your skills and confidence, be open to the parts that appeal to you least. The things we resist most vigorously frequently hold the potential to be our greatest blessing.

You don't need to do everything I suggest. If you implement only one practice or one idea, and integrate it fully into your life and business over the next 12 months, you will make a significant change to your future. A small change sustained over time is far more effective than attempting to implement too much at once and stopping soon after you've begun.

My Prayer for You

My prayer for you, as you work through this book, is that you will be empowered to contribute your unique gift to the world, grow to maturity the business that is already within you, and experience the fulfilment of your heart's desires.

May you step into partnership with Higher Consciousness, let go of struggle, and experience the power of love to transform your life and the lives of everyone around you.

May you be blessed beyond your wildest dreams. May you be the blessing you are destined to be.

> Always remember that you are unique and precious. The world NEEDS you and your gifts.

PART I
Growing Your Relationship with the Universe

A foundational practice for *Growing Business with Soul* is developing a relationship with the Life Force that is as deep and intimate as that between a mother and her unborn child, and allowing the wisdom of that Higher Consciousness to guide you and grow your business.

I'm not suggesting that you accept what is written here just because I say so. I am, however, asking you to be a good scientist, keep an open mind and experiment with the ideas and practices that I offer in this book. Take particular note of how you feel and how you act as a result of engaging with the ideas, meditations and exercises.

I suggest that you adopt a *What if this were true?* attitude to the ideas you will read here. Try them out for size and adjust them until they fit. Experiment with the exercises and meditations and see what evolves for you. You will inevitably adapt and discard ideas and practices as you evolve your own 'working spirituality.' This is as it should be.

Chapters 1 & 2 lay the conceptual framework for the practices that follow. We begin with a quick overview of what the discoveries of new science are telling us about the nature of the universe.

CHAPTER 1
Living in a Conscious Universe

We live in a time of evolving understanding of the universe and our place in it. Old scientific models are being challenged by quantum theory, and science and spirituality are drawing closer together. I am indebted to the works of Gregg Braden and Dr. Amit Goswami whose writings make accessible to my non-scientific mind the findings and implications of quantum research.

Understanding the Universe

At this point in history, there are in the world around us three different ways of understanding the universe: those of religion, old science and new science.

Religion tells us that spirit and matter are different. The spiritual world is real, but is fundamentally separate and different from the world of matter. The physical world is sometimes seen as unreal, or as fallen from a pure spiritual world or heaven. 'God' is to be found 'up and out' from the earth.

Old science says that only things that can be physically measured are real. 'God' does not exist. Spiritual experiences happen when certain parts of the brain are stimulated. Consciousness is a product of the brain.

New science based in the discoveries of quantum research, says that everything is conscious. The universe is made of energy that vibrates at different rates. Fast vibrations are invisible to the human eye. Slow vibrations create what we know as physical matter. Evolution happens in response to an underlying intelligence. 'God' is 'under and through' the entire cosmos. The material world emerges out of an intelligent, guiding consciousness.

For centuries, the mystics of all traditions have told us of the consciousness that underlies all creation. As quantum discoveries are now describing the same reality, science and spirituality are reuniting and humanity is ready to embark upon the next great stage of our evolution. No longer will mystical reality be the domain of a few exceptional individuals. We are all invited to interact with this reality for ourselves and to become practical mystics – consciously playing our part in the unfolding of a new world order.

Implications of Quantum Discoveries

Quantum theory studies the very smallest building blocks of matter – the tiniest particles that make up the physical world as we know it.

Some odd things happen at the level of the quantum particle. Experiments show that separated particles are in instantaneous communication with one another, can exist in two places at once, live in the past as well as the future, and have the capability to change both the future and the past through choices in the present.

It is increasingly being realised that the possibilities that operate at the level of the smallest building blocks of matter also operate at the level of human consciousness. *The only difference between those isolated particles and us is that we're made of a lot of them held together by the power of consciousness itself.*[1]

Quantum theory is clearly demonstrating what the sages of all time have told us: that humans are part of a spectrum of both visible and invisible reality that includes the whole cosmos, and exists outside the limitations of time and space; that everything is connected by a shared 'Field of Consciousness'; and the consequences of every emotion, thought and action ripple throughout the universe.

Learning to Create Consciously

New science tells us that physical matter emerges from a sort of quantum 'soup,' in which multiple possibilities co-exist at any one moment in time. From the infinite potential of the universe, a physical reality manifests through the power of choice. Gregg Braden calls this potential reality *The Divine Matrix*. Theoretical quantum physicist Dr. Amit Goswami calls it *Ground of All Being*. I most usually refer to this underlying consciousness as the *Quantum Field*.

Quantum science also tells us that everything in our universe, both visible and invisible, is in fact energy, vibrating at different speeds. There is more

---

1   Gregg Braden *The Divine Matrix* p 210

space than matter inside every atom and, although our world looks solid and unchanging, in actual fact it is constantly 'flickering in and out of form', faster than the human eye can perceive. This is true even of physical things like rocks and trees and our bodies.

If we want to effect change, the implications of this theory are significant. Throughout this book, I talk a great deal about making a conscious choice about what we want to create. Choosing a new reality with our rational mind is only part of the process. Human emotions communicate with the Quantum Field via our DNA. How we feel about something plays a very significant part in what we experience in our day to day reality.[2]

In order to effectively change an outward reality we must change our emotional response to a situation. This involves learning to co-create consciously with the universe and is a foundational practice of *Growing Business with Soul*. We explore it in some detail later in this section.

The Process of Change

Evolution occurs both in steady incremental steps and in occasional quantum leaps from one state of being to another, without any intermediate step. The same is true for us. We grow towards a new possibility by taking small steps in that direction. As we consistently do this and train ourselves to think and to feel in a new way, there comes a point of quantum leap when we bridge the gap between where we are and where we want to be in one evolutionary bound. I guess we reach an internal tipping point where the emotional and mental energy we have created for the new reality has sufficient critical mass to tip the Quantum Field into creating a new physical form.

There is an intermediate stage during the process of conscious creation in which the old and the new potential realities coexist alongside each other. This is frequently quite an uncomfortable time, because all the change is happening at the invisible level, and we need to hold firm to our intention to change our visible reality. It's rather like planting a seed that germinates underground for a long time before shoots become visible in the outer world.

This happens for us both individually and collectively. If we look only at international news media, we will be convinced that the old realities of violence, greed and injustice are stronger than ever. However, there is another, more positive reality, which is clearly emerging steadily, when you know where to look.

---

[2] For more on the implications for daily life of quantum research see Gregg Braden: *The Divine Matrix*.

There is emerging evidence of a significant shift in human consciousness. Millions of people around the world are waking up to who they truly are and taking significant steps towards fulfilling their potential. There will come a point where the collective consciousness reaches its tipping point and the choice of kindness and justice, which has always been our potential, becomes the deciding choice in human consciousness. When this happens, we will experience a new reality taking shape on the international stage.

At the moment we are living in the messy and uncomfortable stage where two contrasting realities coexist. We are all contributors to the underlying field of consciousness, and our physical reality is shaped by the emotional messages each individual sends into the *Quantum Field*.

By reading this book, you have identified yourself as part of the emerging shift of consciousness for humanity as a whole. Choosing to become conscious and clean up your emotional world helps not only you, but everyone on the planet. It is quite possibly the most important work of your lifetime, and is a major focus of this book.

Take 100% Responsibility for Life

The first step of empowerment – individually, and ultimately collectively – is to take responsibility for what we are creating.

Reflecting on his experience in Nazi concentration camps, Jewish psychologist and Holocaust survivor, Viktor E. Frankl, concluded: *Everything can be taken from [us] but one thing: the last of the human freedoms—to choose one's attitude in any given set of circumstances, to choose one's own way.*[3]

Taking 100% responsibility for your life is not about pretending to have control of all the circumstances of our lives. None of us stands alone. The circumstances of each individual life arise from a complex combination of influences, including culture, economics, our unique soul journey, and the mental, emotional, physical and spiritual environment in which we have been raised and are currently living. Our thoughts, words, emotions and actions all have an impact on everything around us. My choices impact you, and yours impact me. Nor is responsibility about assigning blame. It does not mean that things are your fault because they are the way they are.

Taking 100% responsibility for your life means recognising *that in all situations you have the ability to choose your response* – you have response-ability.

---

3   *Man's Search for Meaning*: quoted online at http://www.goodreads.com/author/quotes/2782.Viktor_E_Frankl

Being able to choose our responses means that first we need to recognise that a choice is possible. Many of our reactions arise spontaneously from deep within our being, much faster than conscious thought. Once this instinctive response has occurred, the ego-mind follows up extremely quickly with an interpretation of events that is consistent with our prevailing beliefs about ourselves and life. This emotional-mental groove becomes deeply engrained over time. The first step in becoming conscious is to notice when you have reacted automatically to a situation. Learning to interrupt your emotional-mental groove long enough for consciousness to emerge is a slow task. Be patient with yourself.

Coming to see yourself as part of a conscious universe, and as contributing to every last experience through your thoughts, emotions and words as well as your actions, can be an unsettling experience. Most people resist this concept at first, but once accepted and integrated, it creates great psychological freedom and is an essential step on the road to spiritual and psychological maturity.

Developing co-creative responsibility demands a whole new set of spiritual, mental and emotional muscles that need to strengthen over time. Like any new skill, constant practice is required, along with plenty of regular rest and a change of environment from time to time.

It is okay to move back and forth in your concept of the spiritual realm and understanding of the universe. I know in my own journey I have had moments of regressing when I just needed to relate to the safe 'Father God' of my childhood belief system. Constantly being an adult and choosing to exercise your co-creative responsibility can be overwhelming at first, so take a rest when you need it. In fact I would encourage you to let yourself be a child from time to time.

Let Yourself Be a Child from Time to Time
Many years ago, when my youngest son was a toddler, I took my family to the beach one winter day. A tractor had recently been on the beach, its tyres leaving deep ruts and grooves in the mixture of wet sand and soil at the edge of the car park. Whilst my long adult legs negotiated the depressions easily, they were enormous to my son's little toddler legs, and he tripped and fell repeatedly before I picked him up and carried him onto the sand below.

Sometimes I feel like a toddler tripping on tractor tracks as I negotiate life.

While the perspective of Spirit looks past the ups and downs of human life to the destination ahead, from our human viewpoint they can seem enormous. They can fill our mental horizon, throwing us off balance and tipping us head over heels. It is at points like these that we need to remember that it is okay to ask Higher Consciousness to carry us.

I have learnt over the years that I'm not expected to grow in a perfectly straight line. There are times when I need to ask for everything to be taken care of, when I say 'Stop the world, I want to get off' or 'God, I need a holiday.' These pauses are probably an important part of the integrative process.

So lighten up and take the pressure off yourself. Start your journey from wherever you are now. You will grow according to your own unique pattern and soul's path.

Welcome Not Knowing

You learn to grow in life by asking the right questions, and by experimentation, trial and error. Open up to the questions that are important for you to ask, and be prepared to not know the answers straight away. **Not knowing is an extremely powerful spiritual state**. Be prepared to let yourself stay in the state of *not knowing* for as long as you need. It is an exceptionally important skill to learn.

Not knowing is a state when all doors of possibility remain open. When you are in this state, keep listening to yourself, follow your energy as it flows and trust an outcome to emerge in the best way for you at the best time. Don't second-guess yourself. If you feel strongly that you want to do something, do it. Equally, don't leap to conclusions or try to force an answer.

There have been many times in my life when I have felt guided to take a particular step, and immediately assumed a particular consequence as a result. For example over a period of five years I attempted to build a network marketing business in two separate companies. In both situations I felt clearly guided to take that step. However, neither business was successful and ultimately I left them behind. From a human point of view you could say that I made a mistake or misheard my guidance. I think it is more true to say that I needed all the experiences that those particular decisions brought me. So the step was right, even though the outcome was vastly different from what I had naively assumed it was going to be.

One Step at a Time

Any journey is made one step at a time. You only need to know where to put your foot next. Take that first step and the next one will become clear when the time is right.

Simply because you commit to a conscious spiritual journey, don't expect everything to become clear or easy. In some ways choosing to be conscious is harder than living unconsciously. Once you have opened your mind to a new idea, you can't go back to not knowing it. Paradoxically, your challenges may become greater as you move forward in this new way of being, but as you open up to what you are capable of and move into fulfilling your potential, I can promise you that your satisfaction and fulfilment will become exponentially greater.

Main Points of This Chapter

- Science shows that everything in the universe is made of energy and arises out of a unified field of consciousness – the Quantum Field.
- Our emotions communicate with the Quantum Field via our DNA to create our reality.
- To change what is happening in our lives, we have to change how we feel about it.
- Taking 100% responsibility for life means learning to choose our outcome by responding consciously to every situation.
- Not knowing is an extremely powerful state.

What This Means for Your Business

Growing your business is first and foremost an inside job. Every part of your life is connected, and your conscious and unconscious emotions are a deciding factor in the degree of success that is possible for you. Your business success is created by your thoughts and feelings as well as your actions.

Cleaning up your emotional life and becoming conscious of your choices are as important to your business outcomes as setting goals, marketing and delivering your product or service.

Grow Your Business Action Steps

Start to notice when you experience a strong negative reaction to something. Take some time to reflect and journal the answers to the following questions. Ask yourself:

- *What did I do as a result of how I was feeling?*
- *What other choice could I have made?*
- *What would have been the probable outcome of the other choice?*

Next time a similar emotion is evoked, see if you can catch the moment before you react automatically and make a conscious choice about your response.

This takes practice – be patient with yourself.

CHAPTER 2
The Power of Love

We now take a look at the nature of the consciousness that underpins the universe.

A Loving Creator?

In keeping with my Christian heritage, a foundational concept of this book is of a Life Force present throughout the cosmos, that can be intimately known and whose nature is love. A short-hand term could be *Loving Creator*. This idea has been passionately believed by millions through the centuries, and equally passionately disbelieved, especially in recent times.

As a teacher of practical spirituality, I would say that the existence of a loving creator can be neither proved nor disproved in absolute terms; however, this belief works to make me more peaceful, loving, kind and hopeful during my time here on earth. And for that reason I think it is a useful framework to keep as part of my 'working lexicon of belief.'

Interestingly, it is a concept being increasingly supported by new science. Quantum physicist Dr. Amit Goswami, gives a comprehensive survey of evidence in the subatomic world which supports the existence of a loving Creative Consciousness.[4]

Describing Love

Love is a central theme of this book, and using it is a core skill that I return to over and over. It is also one of the least understood concepts in current English usage, most usually referring to romantic love, or the love between a parent and child. I choose not to gripe very often, because I find it an unproductive way to be in the world, but if I did have a gripe it would be

---

4 See Goswami: *God is not Dead* for a discussion of the quantum evidence for a Loving Consciousness underpinning all Creation.

the way in which much popular culture here in the West sentimentalises love, turning it into slush with no steel.

In part our difficulty stems from the fact that we have just one word to describe a variety of different types of attachment. Other languages have a greater linguistic variety to choose from.

The ancient Greeks had four words for different aspects of love.[5]

1. *Eros,* romantic love, from which we get our English word *erotic*
2. *Storge,* (store-gay) refers to affection between parents and children
3. *Philia,* the love between friends and equals, was considered a higher level of love
4. *Agape,* (a-ga-pay) is unconditional love that is prepared to sacrifice itself for another, the highest level of all

Agape comes closest to divine love, and was the word used by the writers of the New Testament to refer to the love they saw exhibited by Jesus. But the love I am talking about is even more profound than that.

The Nature of Love

Love is the Creative Force at the heart of the Cosmos. It is the Life Force that underpins and permeates all Creation. You could call it the foundational energy that creates all things and sustains their life, whether that life is in visible three-dimensional form, or invisible form. This love is not always gentle and it is definitely not sentimental.

In his book, *Secrets of the Light,* Dannion Brinkley recounts the spiritual knowledge and understanding which he gained from his visits to the heavenly realms, during three near-death experiences. Here is what he has to say on the nature of love:

Love [is] the most powerful force in the universe. Love is a divine, living energy of unparalleled might and magnificence … For those of us in human form, love is our true state of being … Unconditional divine love … is the force that moves effortlessly throughout the entire universe and through each of us when we allow ourselves to be open channels for its divine expression.[6]

---

5   For an in depth explanation of these concepts see *The Four Loves,* CS Lewis 1958. Available as a free pdf download at *online.santarosa.edu/homepage/jaharonian/TheFourLoves.pdf*

6   *Secrets of the Light* pp 97 – 98

Love Is Natural to Us
We carry the same qualities as the Life Force from which we come. Despite appearances, it is an inherent characteristic of 'humankind' to behave with *kindness*. This instinctive knowledge is reflected in the English language, although few people are aware of it. When we ask: *What kind of bird is that?* we are asking what the defining characteristics of that species are. It is recognised that a particular kind of bird, for example a thrush, will behave in a particular way. The words *kind* (as in 'a kind action'), *kindness* and *kindly* all have the same linguistic root. 'Kindness' is a defining characteristic of 'humankind'. When we act in ways that are 'un-kind', we are acting against our true nature, or in ways that are not typical of our 'kind' or species.

What is Love Like?
My experience is that the essential consciousness which creates and sustains the universe is loving, compassionate and eager to be deeply involved in human affairs. However, it will not violate our freewill, and waits to be invited. Because we are all linked at unseen levels, calling on the power of love to be at work in and through you has the capacity to transform anything that touches you, directly and indirectly. I call this Miracle-Producing-Love and we talk more about it in Part III.

We can identify love by its expression and its effects. Love expresses itself as kindness, compassion, patience, gentleness, and good humour. The effects of love are peace, joy, creativity, resourcefulness and a flourishing of all forms of life. When you call upon love, then you are calling upon the Life Force of the universe to be at work – in you, in what's happening around you, and in the world as a whole.

Love is tough and enduring. Love expects the best. Love will set and enforce boundaries to enable safety and growth. Love transforms. Loving actions arise from the *choice* to love. Humans who consistently choose loving action find that feelings of love will follow. Calling on the power of love is an extremely powerful way to fulfil your divine contract and to be the channel of transformational love in the world that you are destined to be.

Open up to Love
When you really commit to allowing love into your life in a deeper way, you open the door for deep and lasting positive change. When you call upon love, you connect with the potential that is at the heart of every situation, with the essence that is at the heart of every person and at the heart of the universe as a whole. Calling upon love to work through your life and

business turbo boosts what can be created. It's like applying full-strength fertiliser to maximise your growth and your development.

Around the time that I began to work on this book I engaged in a six-week coaching programme with my good friend, Max Ryan,[7] using the mantra *I love myself, I love my life,* on a daily basis. Those six weeks turned into an extremely challenging and transformative stage of my life and business.

Looking back, I can see that by choosing to invoke the power of love in such a consistent way, I created a watershed time, which enabled a whole new set of circumstances to show up in my world.

Love Embraces Everything

It is my consistent experience that love is a powerful force that wants to embrace everything, including the parts of me that I don't like, or would prefer to keep hidden. My husband, Robert, is a professional therapist, who does a lot of work with couples. He teaches that when we commit to love, for example when we get married, the power of love engages with us at new levels, and brings to the surface everything that is not love – *in order to heal it.*

Growing Business with Soul is a way of living that loves you into fulfilling your potential. When you commit your life to be a vessel of divine power in this way, you can expect the things that block the flow of Life Force to come to the surface. Rather than being dismayed and frightened when fear, doubt, and lack show up, rejoice that you are right on schedule in the transformative work of your own being.

As we will discuss later in this section, fear, doubt and lack, especially financial lack, have been part of the collective human experience for several thousand years. When we experience these feelings, it is demonstrating to us something that needs to be healed at both a personal and a collective level.

Every time you choose to let go of your limited human perspective, you open a door for love to be at work. When you find a part of yourself that you are ashamed of or don't like, and choose to love and accept yourself anyway, you open the door to the transformative power of love to be at work in and through you.

By committing to live a life of conscious spirituality, and by doing your own work of inner healing, you are becoming one of the forerunners of

---

[7] You can engage with Max's transformative work at www.attractpositiveresults.com

spiritual evolution for humanity as a whole. Because we are all part of the Life Force, every choice you make to act with kindness, gentleness and forgiveness, assists humanity to shift consciousness away from fear and towards our true nature of love and kindness.

Learning to extend compassion and forgiveness to ourselves and other people is a major part of our soul learning and soul purpose. Even taking small steps in that direction produces miracles, for ourselves and for those around us.

Choosing Love Requires Strength

I have sometimes heard people say that 'faith is a crutch for people who can't manage life by themselves.' In my experience nothing could be further from the truth. Choosing to live as a conscious spiritual being, and to extend the power of love to yourself and all those around you, is the hardest work you will ever do. It regularly demands courage, commitment, focus, diligence, patience and a sense of humour.

However it is also the highest calling, the greatest joy and the source of the greatest fulfilment that is possible. I am so thrilled that you are joining me on this journey of personal and global transformation.

Main Points of This Chapter
- Love is the creative force at the heart of the cosmos.
- Love is the most powerful force in the universe.
- Love is your true state of being.
- It is your destiny to become a clear channel of divine love in the world.
- The practices I will teach you will help you to do this.

What This Means for Your Business

The more you become a channel for love in your business by implementing the practices I will teach you, the greater your impact will be and the more fulfilment and prosperity you will experience. Your life and business will achieve their highest possibility, and you will become a great source of transformation and blessing for the world as a whole.

Grow Your Business Action Steps

Here is a foundational meditation to create your own 'Sacred Centre' deep within the love at the heart of the universe. You can use it as a meditation in its own right or as a place to which you will return for all the other meditations in this book.

Meditation: Resting in the Heart of Love

Instructions are given for sitting in a chair – adapt them if you sit on the floor.

Sit upright with your weight evenly distrbuted, back straight and both feet flat on the floor. Allow your hands to rest palm down on your thighs. Feel your body sitting. Breathe deeply and slowly and allow your body to relax.

Gently close your eyes and turn your attention to your breath. Breathe gently and deeply into your abdomen, relaxing more and more on each out breath.

As you breathe and relax, bring your attention down – into your heart – into your hips – into your legs – into your feet – and into the earth.

Imagine that you are floating down into a beautiful orb of gold and white light that is deep in the earth. Feel yourself filling with peace and serenity as you allow yourself to be surrounded and filled with this gentle, loving presence.

Allow yourself to rest in the heart of this loving light. Imagine that your body, the space around you, your mind, your emotions, are all being filled with this golden light, peace and calm. Invite love to do a deep work in you.

Release all your concerns and responsibilities to the power of love. Allow it to flow into every aspect of your life – bringing about the very best for you and everyone connected to you. Speak any prayers you may wish – or remain in silence.

Stay in this presence for as long as you wish – then gently breathe your awareness back up through your feet, your legs, your body and into the room you are in.

Open your eyes slowly and bring back with you an awareness of the invisible energy of love permeating every cell of your being.

Download an MP3 version of this meditation at
www.JasmineSampson.com/bookresources

Having established the conceptual frameworks, the rest of the book explores the practices that will empower you to grow your business with Spirit as your partner.

CHAPTER 3
Meditate Daily

Prayer and meditation are frequently spoken about together. I have quite a lot to say about both so have given them separate chapters.

Every plant needs deep roots in order to grow strong and be fruitful. A time of daily stillness and quiet is an essential life practice for everyone who is *Growing Business with Soul*. Sometimes you will mostly meditate during that time, while other times you are likely to spend more time praying, and sometimes you will do both. Any combination of prayer and meditation is fine and will change for you from day to day and year to year.

I am frequently asked about the difference between prayer and meditation. Both are spiritual practices that build your relationship with the Life Force. Meditation is most frequently described as *listening* whilst prayer is described as *talking*.

Just as in your human relationships, you get along best when you listen more than you talk!

Why Meditate?
As a busy entrepreneur, your time is your most precious asset. It is very tempting to think you are too busy to take this time for yourself. Let's start by taking a look at some of the key reasons why you are simply too busy *not* to meditate.

Research into the physiological effects of meditation began in the 1970s and continues to the present day. Here is a quick overview.

Meditate for Health
Last year I had a client arrive who had been on medication for anxiety and depression for 12 years. I taught him a simple breathing meditation in the first session, which he practised diligently for ten minutes every day during his lunch break, and again in the evening at home. He came back two weeks later totally transformed, came off his medication and needed only half the number of coaching sessions we had originally scheduled. The meditation made all the difference.

Regular meditation improves your ability to relax, gives you more energy and better sleep, reduces high blood pressure and cholesterol levels, decreases the workload on your heart and strengthens the immune system.

Could your business benefit from your being in great health?

Meditate for Clarity and Focus
Research into top performing executives and business leaders show that they all have a daily habit of shutting their office door and taking 20 – 30 minutes of silent reflection.

People who meditate regularly demonstrate a greater sense of purpose, focus and clarity. They are more able to use their whole brain for problem-solving and are more creative, resourceful and flexible. They also show improved memory and learning ability.

Would thinking clearer and smarter be of benefit to your business?

Meditate for Emotional Resilience
Sally was surprised when a psychometric test came back saying she had been under extreme stress over the last three months. That wasn't how she'd experienced her life at all. However when she thought about what had happened in the previous quarter, she recognised that indeed she had been under a lot of pressure. However, her longterm practice of daily meditation had meant that she did not experience stress.

Would your business benefit from your being calm and resilient when under pressure?

Meditate to Improve All Your Relationships
Research shows conclusively that regular meditators are happier and more peaceful, with greater joy in life and noticeably better relationships with other people.

As one of my students said to me: *'I don't know what it is, but when I meditate regularly I go from being grumpy Dad, to nice Dad. It really is amazing!'*

Would your family, staff and clients like you to be happy?

Meditate To Get More Done
As another of my students put it *'Daily meditation is making it so much easier to focus and I am handling my workload with far less stress than before.'*

Can your business afford for you to be performing at anything less than your best?

It is fairly obvious from this list that any business owner will benefit from daily meditation. However, there are more compelling reasons for those who really want to *Grow Business with Soul*.

Meditate to Tap into the Life Force
The need for silence, and stillness, and peace is as old as we are—and while the voices that compete for our attention and energy may be more sophisticated and intrusive now, they have been there throughout human history.

The Book of Psalms likens the person who takes time to nurture their relationship with the Life Force as being like a tree whose roots go down deep into the underground streams. (Ps 1:3). When storms and drought come, because they are tapped into a source of eternal nurture, their roots hold strong, and the tree holds fast. While the leaves may blow off and a few branches snap, the tree stays standing and will blossom again.

Meditate for Wisdom and Guidance
Meditation is about making time to reconnect with your divine essence and listen to your soul. As such it is an essential step in getting guidance. It is about connecting with your own heart, and learning to hear and follow the deep wisdom that is in you. It will enable you to gain clarity and chart the simplest and most effective course of action through the multiple demands of your day.

The only way you can chart your course with any certainty through all the competing currents of our world, is to stay tuned to your inner voice and aligned with your own spiritual compass. The voice of your Higher Consciousness is a still, small voice. It doesn't shout, it doesn't overwhelm, and it will not be heard above the din of competing voices in the marketplace. This voice, this wisdom and knowing, can't be heard *unless you make time* to get still and open up to it.

Meditate to Become Attuned To The Frequencies Of Spirit.

As we discussed in Chapter 1, we are living in a universe which is made up of energy vibrating at different rates. Visible things vibrate slowly, while invisible things vibrate quickly. Heavy emotions vibrate slowly and happy ones vibrate quickly. The human world is full of 'heavy' emotions: greed, unhappiness, sadness, fear, anger, violence …

The heavy frequencies of negative emotions, critical thoughts, stress and the general debris of modern living bombard your body, cloud your perceptions and undermine your immune system. They literally drag you down to vibrate at the same level, unless you make a conscious and deliberate effort to stay attuned to the higher frequencies. Without this conscious and deliberate attunement to finer frequencies, you set yourself up to function at less than your best and make it very difficult to receive the wealth of support and guidance that is available to you.

Meditate to Fulfil Your Potential

Being spiritually aware is great. But by itself it is not enough. You need to meditate and pray in order to tap into your source of inner nurture – to listen to the voice that guides you surely and quietly along the easiest path of life, to get acquainted with who you really are, and what is most true to your heart. It will help you to make wise decisions and know what to say *yes* to, and what to turn away from.

For life to be as easy and wonderful as it is designed to be—as you *long* for it to be—you need a daily time of silence and stillness just as you need to nourish your body with food and water each day. It is this time of silence and stillness that will develop your spiritual skills and maturity, enable you to listen, understand and act on your guidance, nurture and encourage you when you are under pressure and provide an inner sanctuary of refreshment for you to draw on throughout your day.

And that is why you need to meditate. Every day!

Two Major Types of Meditation

During my training as a Spiritual Director, I learned that there are two major paths to Union with the Divine: the *Way of Emptiness* and the *Way of Fullness*.

The Way of Emptiness aims to bring one into inner stillness and silence by focusing the mind on the breath and/or on a repeated phrase or mantra. Zen Buddhism and many Eastern Meditation traditions use this method.

The Way of Fullness uses visualisation and imagination to focus the mind and emotions. It is often an easier way for beginners, and for some people, it will always be the way that suits them best. Other people begin with this path and then naturally find themselves drawn to the path of stillness and silence as their spirituality develops and matures.

Imagine a mountain with a number of paths leading to the top. Some of these paths meet up partway, some don't, but they all eventually lead to the top. It really doesn't matter which path you are on. So long as you stick to it and keep walking, you will reach your destination.

If you already have a mediation practice that is working for you, fantastic! Keep doing it!

If you have been struggling to perform a breath-based meditation for some time, you may find it easier to try a Guided Meditation instead. *The Inner Light Meditation* at the end of this chapter combines breath focus with visualisation and so will be suitable for just about everyone.

If you are new to meditation, I've included some tips and advice below.

Tips to Make Your Meditation Easier
1. Schedule a regular time in your diary
You won't find the time—you have to *make* the time. It takes 3-4 weeks to create a new habit and 90 days to lock it in. You learned to shower, clean your teeth and dress every day. Think of meditation as daily hygiene for your heart and mind and soul. In the overall scheme of life, 20 minutes isn't much out of your day. But as you have seen, the return on your investment is life-changing and priceless.

If you are very new to meditation, start small, perhaps just five minutes a day, and build up slowly to 20 minutes a day or even more. Block it into your planner or diary as an appointment with yourself. Make it top priority, and if necessary enlist your family and/or staff to help. I suggest you use the timer on your phone to tell you when your meditation time is ended.

Ideal times to meditate are first thing in the morning and last thing at night. These make a nice book end for your day. If early morning doesn't work for you – get creative with time. Try your lunch break, or after work before dinner. Beware of letting your quest for the *perfect time* become an excuse not to meditate. In the end, choose a time that looks as though it's going to work and commit to it.

2. Create a meditation space

Even if you live in a condo, find a corner somewhere to create your own meditation space. After using your place regularly for a little while, just going into your special chair sends a signal to your subconscious that you are preparing to meditate. Your mind and body will start to relax and calm down and make your daily meditation practice much easier.

You don't need very much space. My ideas here are simple and can be applied to any sized room.

At the most basic level, all you need is room for your chair or meditation cushion and a decoration or two. You may also wish to have a small table for a vase of flowers or candle, and maybe a picture or photo which is special to you.

The same principles can be applied to dedicating a corner of your office to meditation and reflection.

3. Create little rituals

Having a regular time and space will help greatly to prime your body and mind to relax and focus. You can augment that effect by always doing the same things in the same order. For example close your door, light your candle, wrap yourself in your shawl, and sit down.

Your body and the inner child part of you love routine and will respond by starting to relax when you begin your ritual.

Points to Remember

1. Maintain correct posture

The most important factor is to ensure your back is straight. If you're sitting on a chair, make sure that you have both feet flat on the floor. If your feet don't comfortably touch the floor, put blocks or books under them so they can be flat. Preferably, take off your shoes, especially if they have high heels.

Aim to keep your hips, knees and ankles at right angles (90 degrees) to keep the joints open. This allows the energy of your body to move freely.

Avoid crossing your legs or sitting with your legs stretched out, as this unbalances your spine.

If you are sitting on the floor, make sure that your weight is evenly distributed and both your knees are on the floor. If you can't do this easily, use cushions to support your knees. You may also find it useful to have a cushion on your lap for your hands to rest on.

If you are lying down, ensure that your back is straight.

Adjust until you feel balanced and at ease – *you are aiming for a posture of minimal effort*. Let your hands rest comfortably relaxed in your lap or by your sides if you are lying down.

2. Breathe deeply and slowly into the abdomen

This is extremely important as a health practice anyway. Breathing in for 6 seconds and out for 6 seconds has been shown to create balance and harmony between the different parts of your nervous system and to bring the body and mind into a state of optimal functioning. I suggest you begin all your meditations by first focusing on your breath and consciously relaxing.

Practise feeling different parts of the breathing movement as you breathe: first downwards into the belly as the diaphragm expands, then sideways into the rib cage as the lungs fill, and finally into the top of the chest. This will slow down your breath and make it easier. Reverse the process on the out breath. (If you've done yoga or Pilates, you will already know how to do this breathing.)

You may choose to spend your entire meditation time focused on your breath.

3. The good meditation is the one you sit down and do.

Don't judge the effect of meditation by how you feel during it. Spiritual highs will happen from time to time but they are not your goal. Consider them a bonus. You are building new mental and spiritual muscle and it takes time for the benefits to be felt in your outer world. You are working at the deep and subtle level of your mind and soul – changes are incremental and deep. Be patient and the benefits will become visible over time.

The people around you will probably notice the difference before you do. Marina's teenage son always encouraged her to come to my meditation group if she was feeling reluctant. *'Mum, go! You're so much nicer when you've been to meditation!'*

4. Don't expect to empty your mind.

You won't. What you are doing is training your mind to focus and relax. This will become easier over time, but you will always have some days that are more distracted than others. This is perfectly normal even for experienced meditators. When you find your attention has wandered, gently bring it back to focus on your breath, or on the visualisation in a guided meditation.

It is normal to need to refocus many times during your meditation.

I have given you just one meditation here to get you started. Breath is essential for our physical life, and light is the basic building block of all matter. In bringing our mind to focus upon breath and light we let ourselves rest in the indwelling presence of the intelligence which animates the whole universe.

I suggest that before you begin you set a timer for the length of time that you have set aside to practise this meditation. The timer on my phone works well for me.

Begin by checking your basic posture, back straight and weight evenly distributed, your hands lying relaxed in your lap.

Download an MP3 version of this meditation at www.JasmineSampson.com/bookresources

Inner Light Meditation

This meditation combines a basic breath meditation with visualisation and a mantra.

1. *Sit comfortably upright, with both feet flat on the floor and your back straight. Let your hands lie with the palms facing upwards in your lap.*

2. *Breathe in slowly and gently through your nose and out through your mouth, consciously relaxing on each outbreath. Imagine that you are a candle and all stress and tension is melting away as you breathe out. Aim to breathe deeply into your stomach, and keep your breathing slow and even.*

3. *Gently close your eyes and consciously relax, from the top of your head right down to your feet. Breathe your awareness down – into your heart – into your hips – into your legs – into your feet – into the earth. Return to the heart of the golden light and allow yourself to feel the love surrounding and filling you.*

4. *Once you are established in your breathing, begin to imagine that pure golden light is flowing into your body with each breath. It fills the area around your heart, and then your entire body. Imagine your body beginning to shine with pure golden light.*

5. *Quietly repeat to yourself "I am full of light" for the rest of your meditation time.*

6. *When you notice your mind has wandered, gently bring it back to focus on your breath or on the light, or on the phrase – whichever attracts you most. Do this as often as necessary.*

7. *At the end of your meditation, spend a few moments resting with your eyes closed, allowing yourself to enjoy your state of peace and relaxation.*

8. *Gently bring your awareness back to the room that you are in, before you open your eyes and go about the rest of your day.*

Come out of your meditation by feeling your feet, and stretching gently with your eyes closed. Open your eyes slowly and sit quietly for a few moments. You may like to record any observations you made in your journal. (For more on journaling, see page 33)

As you become familiar with this meditation, you might like to start using the mantra *I am full of light*, as an inward phrase as you go about your daily tasks.

Main Points of This Chapter
- Meditation has multiple benefits: physical, mental, emotional and spiritual.
- All are important for your business.
- There are two major types of meditation. Experiment to see which one suits you best.
- A daily time of silence and stillness is an essential practice for health, happiness and success.

What This Means for Your Business

Can you really afford *NOT* to meditate? The busier you are, the more important it is. Even five minutes focused breathing and relaxation at the beginning of your work day will reap benefits. Just DO IT!

If you already have a meditation that works for you, keep doing it and *look at it as part of your business development.* If you don't, find one. I recommend the Inner Light meditation provided in this chapter or the *Resting in the Heart of Love* meditation at the end of Chapter 2. Both are online in MP3 format.

NB: Developing silence and inner stillness are an essential part of meditation but sitting still isn't. If staying still is a difficulty for you, go to www.JasmineSampson.com/bookresources to download instructions on taking a Walking Meditation.

Grow Your Business Action Steps

1. Schedule daily meditation time into your calendar.
2. Practise taking a few deep breaths and relaxing at regular intervals throughout your day.

Go to www.JasmineSampson.com/bookresources for instructions on how to create meditative moments throughout your day.

Go to www.JasmineSampson.com/bookresources for more meditation suggestions and MP3s

CHAPTER 4
Pray

To follow the analogy I gave in the previous chapter, prayer is the 'speaking' part of your relationship with Higher Consciousness. It is the time for you to declare your intentions, place your requests, pour out your heart, speak words of loving appreciation ... do whatever you would do with your closest human friends and mentors.

Communicate from the Heart
Your relationship with Higher Consciousness is the most intimate relationship of your life. Express yourself in whatever way feels authentic and real for you. Words are one way; silence is another. The deepest prayers of our heart are beyond words. Experiment with song, drawing, movement, writing and anything else that attracts you.

Keep a Journal
I have mentioned writing in a journal several times throughout this book. If you don't already have one, I would recommend very highly that you start the habit of keeping a regular journal. The journal is different from a diary in that it is focused mostly on your inner life. So you might mention having lunch with an old friend, just as you would in a diary, but the focus of your journal entry would be on the impact of that experience on your inner world. For example, you might record an inspiring comment, or an insight that you had, or how you felt seeing this old friend. Perhaps it brought up particularly happy memories, or unhappy ones that you need to work on. This is the sort of material that goes into your journal.

Your journal can be as attractive and decorative as you wish, but it doesn't have to be. Mine is a hard covered exercise book that I buy cheaply from the stationery store. I have a whole collection of them from over the years.

Some people keep a loose leaf binder, perhaps in sections: one for dreams, another for insights, and another for things you're working on emotionally, etc. Start with what appeals to you and is easy to start *right now*. You can refine your system later if you wish.

I offer you 3 simple steps for journaling:

1. Keep it private. This is the most important step of all. To gain most benefit from your journal you need to write whatever is uppermost in your mind, without any anxiety that someone else might read it. So make sure you have a way of keeping your journal private.
2. Keep it simple.
3. Do it regularly.

You don't have to write in your journal every day, but I recommend that several times a week you make time to record your thoughts, your prayers, your insights, dreams and questions. As little as five minutes, taken regularly, will become a wonderful dialogue with your soul that enables you to mine the deep wells of wisdom and creativity of your Higher Consciousness.

Your Own Words Are Best

There are many beautiful and moving messages on commercial cards, and receiving one of them is heart-warming. But I infinitely prefer a few words written directly to me.

It is the same with prayer: use other people's words when they are helpful to you, but aim to communicate from your own heart. I think we pray more for our own benefit than anything else. Source knows what is in our heart – but often we don't know until we take time to examine it. Prayer helps to reveal your true desires and brings clarity and focus to your intentions.

Be Honest

If you are angry, say so. The strongest relationships are those in which pain, disappointment and anger can be expressed openly and received with love. There was a time in my life when I felt as if I had God by the throat and was saying: *'How dare you do this to me!'* Being able to express my rage honestly enabled me to move forward and grow in understanding and acceptance.

Look to Your Own Spiritual Heritage

If there is a religious tradition anywhere in your background I would encourage you to investigate your own heritage to find the treasures there. When stripped down to their essentials all the great traditions speak of much the same truths: that we are spiritual beings, that this physical existence is a shadow of a greater reality, that we return to that reality upon our death and that the great power and love in the invisible realm is available to us on earth.

Look especially for the mystical writers in the great religions. They speak directly of an experience of God, rather than discussing ideas about God, which is the domain of theology. In Christianity, look for the works of such people as Julian of Norwich, Meister Eckhart, Hildegard of Bingen and Teilhard de Chardin, in Islam for Rumi and other Sufi writers, and in Judaism for teachers of the Kabala.

Many modern writers also write inspired and inspiring material. Make it a habit to browse the 'Spirituality and Religion' section of your library and bookshop and leaf through titles that attract you. Notice how you feel as you read these works and if something makes you feel particularly inspired or happy, then write it down and adopt it into your own practice. Look particularly for prayers and meditations that inspire and encourage you.

The advantage of using prayers and meditations from an ancient tradition such as Hinduism, Judaism, Christianity and Buddhism, is that these practices have been used by millions of people over many thousands of years. When you adopt them as your own, you enter into and are supported by the energy stream of all those souls who have used this practice before you and are using it still. It's rather like the difference between running on your own, and running with a crowd of other people. The energy of the group sustains you and will help your development.

For the same reason, keep your eyes open for a local meditation group or something similar that you can join.

Choose Your Outcome

One definition of prayer is 'deliberately chosen, focused intention.' To understand the effectiveness of this, we can look to both ancient spiritual truths and modern science.

As we talked about in Chapter 1, we know that the physical world arises out of a quantum 'soup', which gets shaped into form by our *predominant* emotions, thoughts and words. In every situation, there are myriads of possible outcomes available in the Quantum Field. *Prayer is a way of consciously exercising your power to choose something different from what you are experiencing now*, and harnessing the creative power of the universe to support your intention.

Here are some different ways of praying that I have used to consciously create my desired outcome.

Experiment with the Idea of Covenant

The concept of a divine covenant between the Creator and humanity is foundational to both Jewish and Christian religions. A covenant is a mutually binding agreement between two parties. Both sides have rights and responsibilities that are clearly spelt out in the terms of the original agreement, and both parties have the right to call the other to account if the terms are not being met.

If this idea appeals to you, I encourage you to draw up your own sacred covenant with the Life Force. You could create a lifetime covenant, or make one each year as part of your New Year practices. You could also do one for your business as a whole or for a particular project. I created one for writing this book: my part is to do the writing, Spirit's part is to inspire my words, enable the writing to flow and direct the whole process of writing, publishing and getting the book into the hands of those who need this work.

Be Willing to Demand

A covenant is a very intimate relationship. The Book of Psalms has a whole section known as the Psalms of Lament, in which the writers tell YHWH, in no uncertain terms, that things are not right on earth, and demand divine intervention.

I have my own vivid experience of the power of demanding from God as my covenant partner.

It was 1998 and I had been single for some time, following the death of my first husband in 1994. For a long time I had wondered if my spiritual calling was to be single, but after four years being on my own, I realised that I had come to the end of the growth that I could do as a single woman, and needed to be in a relationship in order to thrive.

I knew that I was looking for a spiritual companion as well as life companion. It was before the days of Internet dating sites so I tried the available channels, such as advertisements in the personal column, and 'Dinners for 6', but quickly realised that these were not the right places for me to find a man with the spiritual qualities I was seeking.

I spent some months feeling sad and rather depressed, longing for a partner and feeling hopeless about my chances of finding one. Then I happened to come across some teaching from biblical scholar Walter Brueggeman[8] about the Psalms of Lament. He said that the theology of lament is threefold:

1. Things are not right.
2. It's not my fault.
3. God is a Covenant Partner. Do something!

This spoke powerfully into my situation, and from that point, whenever I thought of my desire for a partner, instead of becoming sad and depressed, I would look at the heavens and say firmly: '*I demand that you do something!*'

I met Robert three weeks later, and we were married later the same year.

By choosing to demand divine intervention, I shifted my consciousness from helplessness to power, and opened up to receive something beyond my human ability to create.

Obviously demanding from Spirit is a strategy to use sparingly. However, when you know that you have done everything you can, and still not had the breakthrough that you need, demand can be a powerful resource.

There is a lot more available to us than most people ever ask for. It is my firm belief that Spirit is *looking for* people who are willing to be helped. The spiritual realm is waiting to pour blessing upon you, but will not violate your freedom – you must *ask* for help.

Your deep desires are the desires of the Life Force trying to create something new through you. It is simply a question of getting your limited human perspective out of the way, asking for help and being open to the outcome that your heart and soul really need and desire.

---

8   Walter Brueggemann, 'The Costly Loss of Lament,' JSOT 6 (1986): 57–71.
For those who are interested in Walter Brueggemann, there are a number of excellent YouTube clips.

The Power of Proclamation

Whilst demand is a strategy for exceptional circumstances, *proclamation* is for everyday use. Proclamation declares spiritual power to be at work in the world, before we see it.

For many centuries, spiritual writers from all traditions have taught about the power of the tongue. Learning to monitor the words that you speak, turning away from negative and fearful thoughts and words towards positive and hopeful ones, is an extremely important spiritual discipline.

Proclamation is an ancient practice that takes this one step further, speaking forth the desired outcome with confidence and conviction, to *open the door* and speed its manifestation into your world. Here is an example of how a close friend put this into practice to help her family.

A few years ago, Helen's 12-month-old granddaughter was suddenly admitted to hospital with suspected meningitis. When she heard the news, Helen, like everyone else in the family, was shaken and upset, and her mind inevitably drawn towards 'worst-case' scenarios.

After a few minutes she realised that this was not helping anyone, and moved into *prayer warrior* mode. Although she doesn't consider herself a religious woman, Helen has always believed in the power of prayer to change lives, and knew it was needed now. She had read somewhere about the power of saying NO! to negative outcomes and proclaiming Divine Power into a situation, and decided to put this approach to the test.

Helen was at home alone, and walked the house proclaiming *'No! No! No!'* over and over again. *'I say no to sickness and claim healing for this child.' 'I claim this situation for good. I proclaim divine love at work in this situation.'* She told me later that at one point she chuckled, sounding to her own ears like an old-fashioned Pentecostal preacher in full cry, but she kept on praying.

After about 30 minutes of walking up and down and proclaiming loudly, she slowly felt a sense of peace returning and knew that her job was done. Sure enough, within 12 hours, she heard that her granddaughter had turned the corner and was on her way back to health. She was discharged a few days later and is now a healthy and lively five year old.

Main Points of This Chapter
- Prayer is a way of developing your relationship with the Life Force.
- Your own words are best.
- One definition of prayer is 'deliberately chosen focused intention'.
- Proclaim the action of Spirit before you see it.
- Spiritual help is available to you, but you have to ask for it.

What This Means for Your Business
Prayer is an important part of growing your relationship with Higher Consciousness. Creating a covenant for your business sends a strong signal to your unconscious mind and to the universe that you are serious about fulfilling your potential and are expecting Divine assistance.

Proclaiming your desired outcome before you see it, shapes your unconscious mind and enables your emotions to come into harmony with the creative power of the Quantum Field. This will make it easier for your needs and desires to manifest into the physical realm.

Grow Your Business Action Steps
Draw up your own covenant with the spiritual realm. What do you commit to? What are you asking the Life Force to do?

1. Research the mystical writings of your own spiritual heritage, or of a spiritual tradition that appeals to you. Write out prayers or meditations that make you feel inspired and uplifted and make them a regular part of your practice.
2. Look for a local meditation and/or spiritual focus group to join.

Go to www.JasmineSampson.com/bookresources for resources for this chapter.

CHAPTER 5
Heal Your Trust in the Universe

Faith and belief are not the same thing. Many people think of faith as an intellectual exercise: saying 'yes' to a certain set of ideas. This is belief, and belief has almost no power to change a life.

To paraphrase Psalm 46: 'when an earthquake happens and your world falls apart, stop, be still and *know* God'. *Know* in the sense that it is used here does not refer to head knowledge, but to a deep and intimate experience – a knowing in the very cells of the body.

When we have deep within us a knowledge of the loving presence of a Higher Consciousness that is intimately involved with every aspect of life, we can live with a whole new sense of safety and peace.

Getting Faith into Your Cells

In their fascinating book, *mBraining,* Grant Soosalu and Marvin Oka explore recent research that reveals that there are brain cells, actual neurons, not only in the head but also in the heart and the gut. Each brain has a different competency and focus of attention. When we are functioning in an optimal way, our Heart Brain sets the direction in alignment with our values and passions, our Head Brain adds creativity to find a path forward, and the Gut Brain provides motivation and courage to take action.

Belief becomes faith when the brains in the head, heart and gut all trust the power of the Life Force within us. When an awareness of divine reality is in all three intelligences, then your whole being can act on that truth.

At the point that faith and trust become interwoven into the cells of your body, you have the faith to move mountains.

Faith develops from experience, as beliefs are put into practice. Intellectual knowledge is not enough, which is why throughout this book I give you exercises and meditations to help you to take a concept and make it available to every aspect of your consciousness.

The Problem of Trust
One of the biggest difficulties for humanity is what I call existential fear.

Humanity has come to expect that struggle, scarcity, suffering and difficulty are the norm here on earth. Some of our major religions teach us that we are separated from God/the Life Force/ Source. This is not true, but it certainly describes how the majority of people feel. We inherit millennia of doubt, fear and belief in separation from the Life Force, encoded into our DNA.

Feeling separated from the Life Force has evoked in humanity a deep sense of fear, grief and abandonment which has become deeply woven into the human psyche over many thousands of years. As well as our own personal difficulties, collectively we inherit the anxiety and distress of our forebears: the fear that the universe will not support us; and the belief that we are alone in a hostile world and must fight and compete in order to survive. Not only do we struggle with this individually, but we are heirs to the collective fears of our family, our culture and our social group, indeed of humanity as a whole. Greed, violence and other destructive behaviours arise directly from the sadness and fear reverberating through our collective psyche.

No one is immune to this challenge. To some degree, all humans have been infected with the virus of fear. We all struggle to greater and lesser degrees. We are spiritual beings, but we inhabit physical bodies.

While our own individual choices play a major part in the experience of life, we are all also affected by the combined mindset of humanity as a whole. It is our collective fear and unconscious expectations that continue to perpetuate the suffering prevalent in our world.

We live at a time of shifting consciousness and, because everything is connected, reducing even a small percentage of your own existential fear reduces the fear in the collective consciousness and helps to heal all of humanity.

Become a Spiritual Alchemist and Help Humanity Heal
In the middle ages alchemists went to great lengths in their attempts to transform lead into gold. By using the meditations and practices in this book, you can become a spiritual alchemist, turning fear and doubt into love, trust and faith. Love, the essence of the Life Force, is the transformational ingredient.

I am particularly fond of Tapping (also known as Emotional Freedom Technique or EFT) which induces the body's relaxation response, calms down the amygdala and rewires the neural pathways which hold on to threat and anxiety. It is an exceptionally helpful practice to make part of your daily life. So is regular meditation. There are numerous studies which show conclusively that regular meditators develop parts of the brain which predispose them to be happier and calmer than those who do not meditate.

Both Tapping and Meditation will help you to heal your existential fear and grow in trust. Here are some specific exercises and a meditation I have created on this topic.

(For a Tapping video and MP3 version of this meditation go to www.JasmineSampson.com/bookresources)

Main Points of This Chapter
- Faith involves getting belief into all the brain of your heart and gut as well as your head.
- We are heirs to the collective fear of humanity as a whole.
- Because everything is connected, your growth in healing your trust in the Life Force helps the evolution of humanity as a whole.

What This Means for Your Business
Every part of your life is linked to every other. To the extent that you hold conscious or unconscious fear, you will limit your potential in business, as well as in every other aspect of your life. Investing time and effort into developing a relationship of intimacy and trust in the Life Force will revolutionise your business and every aspect of your life.

Grow Your Business Action Steps
Set aside some time when you won't be disturbed. Have a glass of water and your journal available. Set your intention to release fear and grow in trust in the universe during this time. You can do this either aloud or silently.

Relax by sitting upright in your chair with both feet flat on the floor, your hands lying open in your lap, and breathing gently and deeply into your abdomen. Ask your body to bring up all the ways you hold fear about life and lack of trust in the universe.

Become aware of all the places where you hold tension or feel any pressure in your body. Starting at the top of your head do a complete body scan, making a note in your journal of all the places that you identify. For each one make a note of the following points:

1. Where is it?
2. If you were going to draw this sensation what shape and colour would you draw?
3. What, if any, texture does this sensation have?
4. Is there any emotion you can identify?
5. Rate the intensity of this sensation out of 10.

Your finished list will look something like this:

- Top of my head: flat grey circular pressure. Feels sad and frightened. 6/10
- Dark grey bar between my eyebrows–feels like a wedge, extending back into the top of the eyeball. Intense pressure, very solid. Angry. 7/10
- Triangular dull green ache at the top of the chest. Flat and dull. Feels sad. 6/10

Continue until you have listed all the physical sensations you can identify. Now continue to the following meditation to help heal your fear and grow your trust.

Meditation: Healing Your Trust in the Universe

Close your eyes and acknowledge all of the fear in your body. Say to all the places that you have identified 'I know you're there. I invite you to let go and receive healing from the universe in this time of meditation."

Quietly repeat to yourself "I choose to let go and trust." Keep repeating this over and over as a mantra during your meditation time. Feel yourself relaxing and growing more and more calm and peaceful.

Now imagine that you are being gently filled with healing light flowing over and through you from the heavens. Allow peace and love to wash through your entire energy field and through every particle of your being, gently dissolving all the fear.

Imagine yourself in an 'energy egg' that extends at least an arm's length in every direction around you: above and below, in front and behind you, to your left and to your right. Give Trust a colour and allow this colour to fill the entire 'egg'. Feel yourself being filled with peace and confidence.

Close your meditation by imagining golden light straight from the Divine Heart flowing to seal the outside of your 'energy egg' – like an eggshell. See the golden shell glistening in the sunshine. Feel yourself protected and loved inside your 'egg' of Trust.

Claim Your Trust Healing Resources Online
Go to www.JasmineSampson.com/bookresources for resources for this chapter.

CHAPTER 6

Take Your Place in the Global Jigsaw

A while ago, Robert and I lived in England for a year. As part of a business building strategy I had at the time, I would go into the centre of the city, purchase a dozen single stemmed roses, and give them to random passers-by, together with my business card. Handwritten on the back of the card was the message: *'Always remember that you are unique and precious. The world needs you and your gifts'*.

People responded in different ways. I remember two women in particular. One stopped and read the message, and her face lit up. *'Thank you so much,'* she said. *'You have no idea how much I needed to hear these words today.'* She went on her way, quite radiant. I went home knowing that I had been in the right place, at the right time, and doing the right thing. I will remember that woman all my life, and like to think she too will remember me, or better yet the message she was given.

The other woman I remember clearly responded in a quite different way. I approached her as she walked through the city centre, because I could see that she was desperately unhappy and in need of some encouragement.

When I offered her the rose, she looked at it, looked at me and said, *'Why me?'*

'Because you look unhappy today,' I replied.

'I need more than a rose,' she said, and continued on her way, leaving the rose in my hand.

I think of her from time to time, and wonder how she is getting on, and what might have changed for her if she had been open to receiving the gift that had been offered her. When we become willing to receive *any* gift from the universe, however unlikely it seems, we open to receive other things as well. Sadly, saying 'no' to the rose may have kept her closed down to the very help she needed.

The World Needs You and Your Gifts
If you've ever done a jigsaw puzzle, you will know how frustrating it is to find that you can't complete the picture because one piece is missing.

I imagine the world rather like an enormous jigsaw. Each person makes up part of the final picture. It is not possible to discern the overall pattern from one piece alone, or even from several pieces clustered together. All are needed to complete the picture. Even one tiny missing piece has an irreversible effect upon the whole.

In the same way, your experience, perspective, talents and struggles are all part of your unique contribution to the world picture. In fact, many teachers would say that, at a spiritual level, the work that we each do contributes not only to the world, but to the unfolding of the entire universe. You are an essential part of the global jigsaw and if you don't step up to take your place, then nobody else can.

You are here with a divine mandate. Your life matters. The world needs you and your gifts. No-one else can bring your gift in quite the same way that you can. No one else can take your place.

Do What You Are Designed to Do
My Grandfather, Bert Sampson and my Great-Uncle Henry, were very good with their hands. They were good at making things, good at fixing things and Grandpa was quite entrepreneurial.

So, they joined forces to start a manufacturing and repair business in the small town where I grew up. It ran for about 70 years and was very successful in a modest way. In due course, my father, Selwyn, and his brother Alan and cousin Jed, were born. When they were old enough Selwyn, Alan and Jed followed the custom of that time and joined their fathers in the family business. Alan and Jed were also good with their hands, and worked in the business until they retired. They enjoyed what they did and lived long, healthy, happy and productive lives.

My father, Selwyn, on the other hand, was not good with his hands. He loved to read and think and explore ideas. He was not practical, and he struggled all of his life to do the work that was required of him. As a consequence he was frequently ill and often depressed. He retired young but his health never really improved. He developed Alzheimer's disease in his later years and died ten years younger than anyone else in his family.

I sat with him as he lay dying, and had a vivid image that the essence of him was like a piece of watered silk with beautiful and subtle colours, which had been crunched up and put in the back of a dirty, dark cupboard. The world had never really seen his gifts and never been blessed by who he really was.

Sad though I am for my father, and for the loss of what he was destined to give to the world, nevertheless I view this childhood experience as a gift. It has shaped choices that I have made at various points along my life journey. I am passionate about the vital importance of people doing what they are gifted to do, and know that equipping other people to use their gifts and fulfil their purpose is a key part of the work that I am here to do.

How Do I Discover My Life Purpose?

Many people feel anxious and confused about their life purpose. Finding and fulfilling it can feel like an exam that you have to pass or your life will have been a failure.

I have come to the conclusion that life purpose is in fact multi-layered, and encompasses everything from the attitude we bring towards washing the dishes, driving the car and handing over money at the supermarket, through to our vocation and ideal work. Given such a breadth of opportunity, I figure that everyone is going to be fulfilling some aspect of their life purpose all the time.

Your purpose starts first with who you *are* – the special 'you-ness' that you bring to life – and expands out of that being-ness into everything you do.

The first thing to remember is that you don't have to know why you are here in order to be expressing your soul. As you saw in my story about roses in Birmingham, my soul was expressing herself in the choices I made, even at a time of confusion and difficulty. So too, your soul will have been expressing itself throughout your life.

Soul Themes

In my experience, the answer to the question: *'What is my purpose?'* is constantly evolving. Choices you make at different stages of your life affect the possibilities that unfold. When you know what to look for, you are likely to find that there are certain themes recurring in your life–in your relationships, in the things that attract or repel you, catch your interest and arouse strong feelings in you.

While the living out of your soul essence will probably change and develop over a lifetime, the overarching purpose of your life is likely to fall into one of seven great themes. Identifying your overarching theme will help you make wise decisions about the things that you pursue and develop. It will alert you to possibilities that you might otherwise miss, and give you clues about how best to learn and contribute in different situations.

Seven Great Soul Themes[9]

To create — to bring new inspiration into the world: including the creative arts and also everyday creativity, such as creating a beautiful home or garden

To heal — to soothe and reconcile: encompassing healing and reconciliation at a personal level, for oneself, or one's immediate family and community

To lead — to inspire and invigorate: bringing enthusiasm and vision to individuals and groups

To organize — to manage and create structures: providing the foundation on which to build individual and social projects

To teach — to communicate or transmit: including higher wisdom and spiritual truth, and also practical skills and social values

To transform — to act as a catalyst for change: facilitating changes that may be personal and/or social

To protect — to nurture and encourage: stewardship of our planet, caring for children, animals, people who are unwell and heritage projects

---

9 Adapted from the work of Theolyn Cortens: *Working with Your Guardian Angel: a 12 week course for finding life's purpose* p 93

Your theme may be immediately clear to you—one word will attract you above the rest. Or it might be the one you least want it to be. You may find that two or even three things stand out to you. For example I resonate strongly with both healing and teaching. Healing has been dominant in the early part of my life, and I find teaching becoming more prominent as I move into my middle years.

Living Your Soul Theme

Knowing your theme does not prescribe a particular career path for you, but it will suggest to you the easiest and most satisfying aspect of yourself to offer in your business. For instance, a doctor whose primary purpose is healing will probably want to build a career with strong levels of patient contact, whereas a doctor whose primary purpose is teaching would be happier lecturing, or building a mentoring and tutoring component into their practice.

Each of the themes can be lived out in a variety of ways. The way that is best for you may change over time as you grow and develop. It will interact with your life experience as a whole, and your gifts and abilities in other areas. Once you have identified a theme, consider it in more depth. For example if your theme is to transform, are you good with your hands – perhaps a cook or a gardener, or with words – a writer or inspirational speaker?

An Evolving Journey

As I look back now, I can see that the business I was trying to build while we lived in England was never going to be the right thing for me. Although at the time I was fearful and desperately frustrated by my lack of success, now I am thankful that project never took off. If it had, I wouldn't have found my way to the work that I am truly destined to do.

From this perspective, I can see that even though I was out of alignment in terms of how I sought to make a living, my soul essence and soul purpose still continued to express themselves on a daily basis.

My underlying intention was to fulfil my purpose. And so the universe supported and guided me, as I experimented and learnt from trial and error what is right for me and what isn't. The same is true for you.

Your Pain and Mistakes Are Part of Your Unique Contribution

In terms of your unique contribution to the world, the things that you struggle with most are even more important than your gifts and talents and the things you find easy. If you have ever seen a handmade tapestry or piece of embroidery, you will know that the image is clearly visible on the front, but when you turn it over the back can be a mass of knots and stray threads, and it is very difficult to discern the picture.

I think of life as being rather like a tapestry. We look at our life from the back and see knots, tangles, loose threads and a general mess. Higher Consciousness looks at the tapestry from the right side and sees the pattern that is being woven.

Mistakes don't matter. Nothing is wasted in the universal economy. Your *whole* life is what makes you utterly unique and is the soil out of which your potential and purpose grow. If you allow it, everything in your life becomes part of your unique offering to the universe. It's your underlying intention and foundational choices that count.

Main Points of This Chapter
- You are here with a divine mandate.
- Your soul is encoded with a theme to live out.
- You have a unique place to fill in the world.
- No-one else can make your contribution.
- Your struggles and mistakes contribute as much to your unique gift as do your strengths and skills.

What This Means for Your Business
Making the conscious commitment to fulfil your purpose and take your unique place in the world, is a foundational step for shifting your business from ordinary to extraordinary. When you take this step, you enable your soul and the universe to engage with you in deeper ways, and open a door to receive guidance and support, prosperity and happiness at a whole new level.

The more you focus on being an open channel for the expression of Divine Love in the world, the more easily your business will develop. Synchronicity and opportunities will appear more and more often as you develop the skill of working in harmony with a Higher Consciousness.

The path ahead will still have challenges and unforeseen twists and turns, but you will have an underlying sense of peace and security that enables you to meet those challenges much more easily than when you are trying to build your business from your limited human perspective.

Grow Your Business Action Steps

If you haven't already done so, start keeping a journal to record your reflections, insights and experiences. I write about the practice of journaling in more detail on page 33.

Go back to the list of Soul Themes and see which word most appeals to you. Make a note also of any that you are particularly averse to. Strong emotions, both positive and negative, hold important clues to your inner life.

If your soul theme is not immediately clear to you, ask to be shown or guided, and you will receive the necessary direction. Relax by sitting quietly and invite your innate wisdom to alert you to which theme is yours. Be open to what emerges and allow the awareness of your theme to come to you. It may come in an unexpected way, so be alert for words of a song, or a passing conversation 'sticking with you.' You might have a particularly vivid dream, or be strongly attracted to a book or a picture. You could also try asking your friends and those who know you well – they usually see us more clearly than we do ourselves!

Consider the following questions in your quest to deepen your understanding of your soul theme and the overarching intent of your life:

1. What is it that you find yourself doing over and over again in different ways and different circumstances? This is a major clue to what your soul wants to express.
2. Are there unlikely gifts that the universe is offering to you right now? Be open to receive whatever is offered to you, even if it doesn't seem to be what you need or think you want right now. Remember that staying open to receiving will move you forward.
3. Is there something you have been trying and consistently failing to achieve over a period of time? Consider the possibility that this is not the right thing for you. Perseverance is a wonderful character trait, but the thing that is right for you will feel natural and give you a sense of satisfaction, even in the midst of challenges. If it doesn't feel like it fits you, or you are consistently unhappy with what you are doing, then it's probably not the thing you are here to do. Let it go!

Meditation: Taking Your Place in the Global Jigsaw

If you haven't meditated before, I suggest that you review my advice about how to meditate on page 27 before you begin.

This meditation is in two parts. You may pause after Part 1 or repeat it one or more times before you move on to Part 2.

Begin with three deep cleansing breaths, in through the nose and out through the mouth, relaxing more and more deeply on each outbreath. Allow yourself to relax more and more deeply into the chair, into the floor, into the earth. Float down into a beautiful orb of golden light deep in the earth.

Focus your awareness into your breath. Notice the rise and fall of your belly and chest as you breathe and relax.

You become aware of a light inside you. You will find your own instinctive place somewhere in your chest where the light is emerging. It grows brighter and brighter with each breath, and you feel more and more calm and relaxed. Light is shining around you in every direction, as far as your mind's eye can see: beautiful light, calm, refreshing, and still.

You feel more and more peaceful, comfortable, relaxed and alert.

In your mind, quietly repeat to yourself 'I choose to fulfil my divine purpose.' Repeat this phrase over gently and quietly to yourself: 'I choose to fulfil my divine purpose.'

As you repeat these phrases, and anything else that feels right to you, over and over gently and quietly in your mind, you slowly become aware that you are moving effortlessly. In your mind's eye, you become aware of the divine pattern being woven through the universe. You are aware of a great sense of order, and can feel the power of divine love resonating underneath everything you can see.

You may wish to stop your meditation here and rest in divine love. Keep repeating this first part until you sense clearly the divine pattern and are ready to move onto Part 2.

Imagine you are looking down from above upon an enormous, multi-dimensional jigsaw puzzle. You see a space below you, and instinctively know that this is your place. This space stands out to you, it shines with bright light, and you feel yourself irresistibly drawn towards it.

You draw closer and closer, and with a sense of great delight you find yourself slipping effortlessly into place. You can feel the solidity and security of being in your divinely appointed place in the unfolding universe. You are filled with a quiet joy, and a sense of having come home to who you truly are, and to where you are meant to be.

You feel the support and safety of the other pieces around you. You know in every fibre of your being that you are loved totally and completely, highly valued and treasured, just as you are. There is nothing that you have to do. Just being who you truly are, is enough. You feel calm and deeply peaceful.

Let yourself rest in this wordless knowing. You can feel the energy of your divinely appointed place soaking to the core of your being. As you rest here, you are becoming more and more aligned with your true nature, with your soul essence, with the place that is yours in this world.

Let yourself feel the resonance of your unique note in the music of the spheres.

Your mind, your emotions and your body are deeply refreshed as you let yourself rest in the place that is yours in the universe.

Finish your meditation by resting quietly, or asking for guidance or words of wisdom and encouragement. If you wish you may repeat quietly to yourself: 'Thank you. It is done. Amen.'

When you are ready to end your meditation, bring your awareness fully into your body, feeling your feet on the floor and stretching and connecting fully with your body before you open your eyes.

Rest quietly for a few minutes before going about the rest of your day. Make a note in your journal of anything that occurs to you, either during or straight after this meditation.

The more frequently you use this meditation, the more your being will become attuned to the vibration of your unique contribution, and your life and business will start to form themselves around that frequency.

You can download an MP3 version of this and other meditations in this book at www.JasmineSampson.com/bookresources

Alternatively, you may wish to record the text for yourself using the meditation as a springboard for your own process. Choose the words that appeal to you most, and go at a pace that is comfortable for you. You may wish to pause or even end the meditation part way through. Trust what feels important to you at any time.

CHAPTER 7
Ask for Guidance

A major aim of this book is for you to become skilled in accessing your own spiritual wisdom and knowledge, and in hearing, understanding and following your own inner voice and guidance.

When it comes to tuning into your inner wisdom to make decisions, otherwise called *seeking guidance*, it really is a case of use or lose it. We are all born with a strong connection to our inner knowing, but because most of us have not grown up in a society which has taught us how to recognise and act on our inner wisdom, this ability tends to lie dormant and is largely unused by most adults. A few lucky people have had mothers or mentors who taught them to develop this innate skill. A few others are blessed with the confidence to trust their intuition, but most of us have room to grow in this area.

Like any new skill it takes practice – and the more you practise, the easier it becomes. Just like learning to walk, you will tumble sometimes. Set the intention right now that you will be kept safe by Spirit and on the right path; and that the right doors will open for you and the wrong ones be shut.

Guidance Is an Everyday Issue
I suspect that the reason most people don't ask for guidance on a more consistent basis is that they think it is about great big decisions such as whom to marry, what job to take or where to live. Certainly, the more far-reaching the impact of the decision, the more important it is to seek out the wisdom of your Higher Consciousness. However, the guidance I'm talking about is much more foundational than just those big, life-changing decisions.

Everyday life is full of decisions. Which route shall I take to town to avoid traffic congestion? Do I have time to make this phone call before I finish work for the day? What shall we have for dinner tonight? Shall I pursue this business opportunity or let it go?

Align with Your Inner Knowing

Big decisions tend to arise out of little decisions, and the cost of being out of alignment with your inner knowing can be very high indeed. I remember watching *Dr. Phil* work with a young couple who had been unhappily married for several years. Their home life was a constant pitched battle creating huge unhappiness for themselves and their children, and their mutual animosity and distrust was overflowing into the television studio.

Dr Phil asked the young woman, 'At what point did you know something was wrong?'

'The night before our wedding,' she replied.

He said, 'You didn't listen to your intuition then, and this is the price.'

In actual fact, I would be sure that she received many nudges from her intuition about this relationship long before it got to the wedding. But she had ignored them and her whole family bore the consequences.

There have been at least three times in my life when it seemed to me that I was being asked to take a step that seemed exceptionally risky to me. It both fascinated and terrified me at the same time. With my knowledge now, I realise that the voice of Spirit doesn't produce that sort of response in us. But I didn't know it then. In each case, when I knocked on that door – tried to take the step I believed I was being guided to take – the door would not open. Circumstances did not allow me to take that step. I look back now and am profoundly thankful that those paths did not open to me. My intention to be faithful overrode the confusion I was feeling and my difficulty in interpreting my guidance.

Committing to follow your guidance brings you into alignment with the constant flow of the Life Force in your unconscious mind. It enables life to become an adventure of delightful surprises. A simple example happened one morning when I 'happened' to walk out of my office door just in time to meet a woman who was waiting to see a colleague who works in the same building. She had picked up one of my pamphlets to read while she waited and wanted to ask me about healing for her daughter.

As you progress you will develop your own attunement to the spiritual realm and your own particular ways of receiving guidance. To get you started here are some suggestions and tips.

Four Principles of Guidance
1. *Higher Consciousness speaks through circumstances, and common sense.* Look for the small, simple and obvious solution first.
2. *The right path opens easily.* Your life is designed to be flowing. If you have to constantly push and strive at something, it is not the right path, or it is not the right time. I have learned to 'knock on the door' twice only. If a particular course of action does not open at the second attempt, then I walk away.
3. *One step at a time.* Learn to walk in trust. Rather than having to see the whole road ahead in advance, learn to take the step that is in front of you, and know that once it is taken the next one will become clear.
4. *To decide between different options: Choose the one that makes you feel most expanded and open.* Tune into your body, especially around your heart, and consider the options one by one. Notice what changes around your heart. This is an excellent general guide and applicable to just about everything. For example, I use this when out driving to decide on the best route through traffic.

Testing the Messages
A useful guideline I have used for many years in assessing whether something is useful to me or not, is to ask myself: *'Does this person/situation/idea/opportunity open me up or close me down?'* If I feel more open-hearted, generous, confident, courageous, loving and kind, then I proceed with confidence. I choose to avoid people, ideas and situations that make me feel more closed, fearful, suspicious or critical. These are not the hallmarks of Spirit. They do not contribute to my happiness or growth and have negative effects for those around me.

The quality of the feeling that comes with a message/decision/thought is your guide to its authenticity. *Peacefulness and the easy flowing of practical steps are key signs that you are on the right path.* As a general guide, ask yourself how this person/idea/possibility/place makes you feel, or what you observe in this person.

Trust ideas, things and people which have some or all of the following characteristics.[10] They make you feel or are:

- Peaceful
- Consistent
- Loving
- Patient
- Uplifting and gently expansive
- Instructive
- Comforting
- Clear
- Kind
- They welcome scrutiny and questions.
- They seldom need to be responded to in a hurry.

These are symptoms of states of higher consciousness.

Be wary of things that:

- Want to make you look good in your own eyes or in front of other people
- Appeal to vanity or self-interest
- Are a logical conclusion of your own learning or thinking
- Vary depending on what information you have received or how you are feeling

These come from the ego (small human, separated self) and are not the highest path.

Avoid anything that is characterised by any of the following states, which come from a lower consciousness, and do not have your best interests at heart. These states:

- Accuse, and/or produce guilt
- Create confusion
- Promote fear and panic
- Become angry or bluster, belittle or confuse when questioned
- Insist there is only one right way to be or do something
- Create anxiety and are generally unsettling
- Are pushy, urgent, wanting to be done in a hurry–a driving compulsion to 'do it now'

---

10 Adapted from Paul Hawker: *Soul Survivor*

(Note that many sales messages have these characteristics, and so do some religious ones!)

If in doubt, ask for clarity and wait for peace. There are few emergencies in the spiritual realm and things seldom need to be done in hurry. When you follow your guidance consistently, you will know and trust when you are on your highest path.

If you must act now, ask for any action that you take to be used for the highest good for all, then do your best.

Remember, it is your intention that carries you through and enables the highest possible outcome for everyone concerned to emerge from the Quantum Field.

Main Points of This Chapter
- Guidance is an everyday issue.
- You must follow it or you'll lose the ability to hear it.
- The right path opens easily.
- Peace is the hallmark of guidance from Spirit.
- Intend to be on the right path and you will be kept safe.

What This Means for Your Business
The more you are willing to be guided by Spirit, the more easily and joyfully your business will develop. Your regular practice of meditation, prayer and the other exercises in this book will all help to refine your sensitivity to nudges from Spirit.

Grow Your Business Action Steps
1. Take a few minutes to centre and tune in before you write your 'to do' list for the day.
2. Use the written meditation below when you are setting your 90 day goals.
3. Make peace your guide. When you find you aren't at peace, stop what you're doing and check in with Spirit. Ask to be guided back to the right path. Follow the prompts.

Meditation for Guidance

When there is something particular on which you would like guidance, try making a written meditation. The instructions are given below.

Set yourself a specific length of time: 15-20 minutes, including writing time, is a good length when you are starting out. Have your journal and a pen beside you.

1. Choose a particular question or questions that you want advice on and write them in your journal before you begin.
2. Relax and breathe your awareness down through your body, into your legs and into the earth. Connect again with your sacred centre in the heart of the gold and white light. Once you feel settled in your centre, ask your question, then immediately record any impressions and thoughts that come to you in reply. With practise, this will become easier.

Trust what you are given and write without censoring. I find that when I write the first phrase that comes into my mind, more comes. If I don't write, I don't get anything else!

Go to www.JasmineSampson.com/bookresources to download this meditation and other resources for this chapter

CHAPTER 8
Harness the Power of Intention

In his superb book *The Power of Intention,* the late Dr. Wayne Dyer described intention as the creative principle of the universe. He tells us to:

'... dwell on the idea of the supreme infinite power producing the results that you desire. This power is the creative power of the universe. It's responsible for everything coming into focus. By trusting it to provide the form and the conditions for its manifestation, you establish a relationship to intention that allows you to be connected for as long as you practice this kind of personal intent.' [11]

This book is about allowing yourself to relax into the creative power of the universe and allow the business potential that is inscribed on your DNA to express itself. It is about letting go of the ego and its preoccupations and limitations, and opening up to a power greater than your human self. When you surrender into this power and harmonise your human intention with the divine intention, your life and business takes on a whole new dimension of beauty, power and effectiveness.

Opening up to Divine Intention

There is a stream of energy, a cosmic vibration, which is uniquely yours. When you choose to use your free will to harmonise your life with divine intent, this vibration will flow through you into every aspect of your human life. When writing this book, I struggled every time I tried to *think* what I wanted to tell my readers. But when I let myself trust, opened my heart and my mind and simply allowed myself to speak the impressions as they came

---

[11] *The Power of Intention:* Wayne Dyer p36

to me, words began to flow. Editing is still needed, but the words flow much more easily when I intend to connect with a higher mind and this ease and flow is not possible when I try to write from the limitations of the ego-mind.

Artists, musicians, writers, and inventors all describe similar experiences of opening to something bigger than themselves and allowing the creative endeavour to come from a place beyond their limited human consciousness.

The same principle applies to you, whatever your contribution to the world might be. You might not think of yourself as creative in a traditional sense, but your life and business carry the imprint of your unique energy signature. Growing your business is a creative act, just as much as any painting. Intend to grow your business supported by a power beyond the human realm.

Expand Beyond Your One-Pixel Mind

I explain to my clients that our minds are like a picture made up of 1001 pixels. Our conscious rational mind is just one pixel, the unconscious and subconscious minds make up the other 1000.

Most people are trying to build their life from their one pixel mind (also called the ego-mind[12]) and wondering why the results they are getting are not what they wanted. Trying to manifest from the limited reality of the rational mind is a frustrating exercise. The logical brain simply does not have enough awareness of the multi-layered aspects of energy that make up the conscious and unconscious aspects of your being. Nor can it assess the ripple effects your choice will have on the invisible fabric of Life itself. But your expanded consciousness can. Detach from the outcomes that your ego-self wants. Use the power of intention to step beyond the limitations of your one pixel mind and allow the creative energy accessible in the ever-creating consciousness of the Life Force to flow through you.

Intend that everything in your life is harmonising within a greater plan and that all you have to do is hold firm to your intention, relax and allow it to

---

12 I use the term ego or ego-mind to refer to the part of us that is convinced we are separate from everything else. The ego is ruled by fear and limitation, and can only make decisions based on what it has already experienced. This part of us is severely limited and learning to expand beyond it is essential for growth and happiness in life and in business.

It's not that the rational and logical brain is to be ignored – but it is to be put at the *service* of your intuitive wisdom and expanded consciousness. In the west, the linear logical left-brain has been given predominance. It's become the boss instead of the servant. This has led to great imbalances in Western culture that we are only just beginning to outgrow.

happen. Trust that you are being guided to the correct actions at just the right moment.

Intend to be balanced within the flow of giving and receiving that is at the heart of universal flow. If it feels that you are giving too much, let yourself relax to receive. If it feels like you are not giving enough, allow energy to flow out through your hands and heart. Let yourself come back into balance in relationship with the universe.

Entering Your Unique State of Flow

The opposite of struggling and striving is something that Mihaly Csikszentmihalyi[13] calls *being in flow*. It is a powerful state where you are exercising your free will to intend that you live a connected life.

Each person gets into flow in a different way. Some people run, others fish. Still others walk in nature, or listen to music chosen for its ability to support a state of 'connection.' Others dance. For me getting into flow involves entering a state of light meditation. I need to close my eyes and shut out the world around me, let go of the critical voice, and simply allow something to come through me. When I am in that state I feel a deep sense of peaceful expansion and a quiet joy.

As an expression of the divine life force, you are gifted with the same qualities as the divine spirit. Wayne Dyer identifies these qualities as creativity, kindness, love, beauty, ever expansiveness, abundance and receptivity.[14] The hallmarks of being connected to your true self are gentleness, peace, happiness, trust and love. The more you practise the skill of staying connected to your soul intention, the more clearly you will recognise your own unique frequency and reveal it in your life.

Manifesting your Heart's True Desires

Being in your unique state of flow will represent a fulfilment of your deep heart's desires. I have always desired to be able to live and express myself from this state of connection. It has taken many years of learning to let go of the restrictions of my ego self to get there. I feel right now that I'm barely dipping my toes in the water, but I rejoice that I have finally reached the ocean shore.

---

13 Csikszentmihalyi is noted for his work in the study of happiness and creativity, but is best known as the architect of the notion of *flow* and for his years of research and writing on the topic. He is the author of many books and over 120 articles or book chapters. His works are influential and are widely cited.

14 *The Power of Intention* pp 42 – 55.

What is it that you have glimpsed throughout your life? What possibilities has your heart responded to? How do you consistently want to feel? The clues to your soul keep showing up in your life over and over again as dreams, desires and longings recurring consistently over time.

The sculptor Michelangelo said that the magnificent figures that he sculpted already existed intact inside their own piece of marble. His task was simply to remove the outer layers of rock to reveal the figure inside. We are the same. Every time you meditate and connect with what your soul desires to experience and express in this life, you are moving to fulfil your potential. Every time you release fear, judgement, or any other negative emotion, you are chipping away the excess marble to reveal the beautiful being that lies at the centre of your heart. By practising the power of intention you will manifest your heart's true desires, not what your ego-mind thinks it wants.

Your Effect on Other People

We have already considered how powerful it can be to focus on the *feel* of your soul energy and allow the wisdom of Higher Consciousness to choose the best vehicle to manifest that vibration in your life.

The next key is to focus your awareness not only on how you wish to feel, but in *how you would like others around you to feel* as well. You are not here in isolation. You are intimately connected to every particle of the universe, and most obviously and closely to the people close to you, including those who are served by your business. Becoming clear about the effect you want to have on everyone around you anchors your intention securely in the manifest reality of your everyday life. Recognise that you both give and receive energy from your entire environment and intend to be blessed, *in order to be a blessing for the world around you.*

I know that I desire to feel free, joyful, fulfilled and light. I wish my body to be full of vitality and health. I aspire to be in harmony with my unique vibration and allow that to flow strongly through me into the world. And I desire the same things for my students and clients and the people around me. I love to assist others to their highest vibrational state and to receive from them the same assistance.

This insight about the deepest desires I hold for myself and other people came to me as I sat in a light trance, allowing this book to flow through me. I would recommend that you let yourself go into a similar meditative state and be open to an awareness of what you most truly desire to form within you. Set the intention that, as you identify these soul longings, you will be manifesting them more and more clearly in every aspect of your life.

Choose a Direction and Allow Spirit to Get You There

A repeated small change can create an enormous shift over time. Imagine a red car and a blue car travelling exactly parallel. If they continue unchanged they will end up at the same destination, a few metres apart. However, what happens if the blue car makes a minute adjustment to its direction? At first this shift is imperceptible, but over time the two vehicles move further and further apart. After a while, the blue car, which made the minor adjustment, is passing entirely different scenery from the red car which has continued on its original path.

Setting an intention is like making a one degree shift in your direction. The change is invisible at first, but maintaining an intention harnesses the creative power of the universe and unleashes deep forces of change which become apparent over time.

I can remember clearly two distinct times in my life when I set a clear intention into the universe.

One was as a new bride aged 23. One evening my husband came home stressed and unhappy, and as I turned to greet him my own mood plummeted, without ever a word being spoken. In that moment, a decision rose up from deep within my unconscious that I was not going to keep letting my emotional life be ruled by other people.

This decision launched me into the major work of my life. Gaining mastery of my own emotional state is a life's work that continues to this day, and constitutes the majority of help I offer to other people.

The second occasion occurred 16 years later, when I was widowed very suddenly at the age of 39, leaving me with three young sons to guide and support. I remember standing in our bedroom the night my husband died, and deciding that, regardless of what life 'threw at me', I was going to thrive and to flourish.

A few days later I was to have one of the most intense experiences I have ever had of the spiritual realm, feeling what I can only describe as a 'golden presence' all around me. I saw myself standing at the top of a high cliff looking across a rocky and thorn-filled ravine, to a sunlit mountain meadow. This place was beautiful, lush and green, full of flowers, trees and birds and a very desirable place to be. I knew that this was where I was headed, although I would first have to cross the difficult terrain that lay between the place where I stood and this beautiful place in my future.

In the weeks and months ahead there were times when I felt that I was face down amidst the rocks and the thorns. Some days it took all my energy and courage just to keep breathing, I could not move forward at all. But I could keep facing in the same direction. Over time, life became easier and I began to experience joy again. I am truly grateful to this experience, knowing that many things I treasure most about myself and my life have their roots in that time.

I am often asked: 'But what if I don't know how to get where I want to go?' The *how* is not your problem. Your responsibility is to use your freewill to choose a direction. Setting your intention is like programming your spiritual GPS for your desired destination. Once you have done that your unconscious mind gets to work to create the path. All you have to do is stay tuned to your inner wisdom and act upon the guidance you receive.

Main Points of This Chapter
- Intention is a powerful way of harnessing the creative power of the universe to assist you.
- Allow the creation of your business to come from a place beyond your limited human consciousness.
- A small degree of change creates a huge shift over time.
- Set a direction and allow the power of the universe to guide you in the right direction.
- In setting your life intention, consider not only what you want to experience, but what you want other people around you to feel.

What This Means for Your Business
You don't have to develop your business relying on human skills and knowledge alone. The same Life Force that creates and sustains the universe is available to empower your efforts, when you ask for it.

Intend to fulfil your potential. Intend to flourish. Intend to be successful. Intend to be joyful and happy. Intend to have more than enough for all of your physical needs. Allow excess possessions and old ideas to flow away. Be grateful.

Grow Your Business Action Steps

1. Each morning, set the intention that today will be a good day. Think yourself through the day ahead, imagining the people you will meet and the tasks that need to be performed. Set the intention that you, and everyone you interact with, will be guided and blessed and that life will flow. Take note of ideas and 'coincidences' that occur. Act on them!
2. Trust your feelings and check in with them regularly throughout the day, as they are your most reliable guide. If you feel 'lightness', or a state of connected happiness, you have remained connected to the power of intention. If at any point throughout the day you notice that you are feeling tense or blocked or that things are not flowing as you would wish, stop and reconnect to the light at the centre of your being. Focus your attention onto your inner light, and reconnect with the peace and tranquillity that radiates from your heart. Allow your mental and emotional energy to relax back into harmony with the timeless peace that is at your core. Watch how your effectiveness and productivity increase as you and everyone around you relaxes and life flows more easily.
3. Imagine yourself moving gently and joyfully through life, with exactly the right combination of events, people, resources and opportunities flowing towards you. They intersect with your life stream at exactly the moment that you need them. Imagine that you can put your hand out and take from the stream of life exactly what you need right now. Be very grateful.

Meditation: Discovering the Power and Beauty Within

If you are new to meditation, before you begin, review the basic instructions on page 28. Begin in your usual way, with your weight evenly balanced, your back straight and both feet flat on the floor.

Breathe deeply and slowly and allow your body to relax as you breathe your awareness down through your body and into the earth. Float down once again into your sacred place at the heart of the golden light of love.

Focus your awareness on your heart centre, near your physical heart in the centre of your chest.

Imagine yourself as a piece of beautiful crystal with a magnificent figure deep at the centre. What colour is your crystal? Surrounding this beautiful figure are layers of stone, some thin, some thick, that obscure the beauty within. Give permission for Higher Consciousness to clear away anything which obscures the beauty and the power that you are here to express. Be willing to let go of everything that does not accurately express who you truly are.

Imagine that you are being filled with golden light that gently dissolves everything that is no longer necessary. Everything that obscures the beauty within is gently dissolving away, and your pure soul intention and soul expression is being revealed more and more clearly every time you do this meditation.

You can download an MP3 recording of this meditation at www.JasmineSampson.com/bookresources

CHAPTER 9
Welcome Your *Shalom*

Thriving instead of struggling is a choice we can make when we decide to live in accordance with spiritual principles. The concept of *Shalom* describes the fulfilment, happiness and prosperity that is the divine intention for humanity.

Allow Your *Shalom*
Shalom is the state of well-being that becomes possible when you choose to live a life governed by spiritual principles. This Hebrew word is most commonly translated as *peace*, but many allied ideas are contained within *Shalom*.

The concept of *Shalom* includes completeness, wholeness, health, peace, welfare, safety, soundness, tranquillity, prosperity, perfectness, fullness, rest, harmony, the absence of agitation or discord. In Modern Hebrew the related word *Shelem* means 'to pay for', and *Shulam* means 'to be fully paid.'[15]

From this list, you can see that the possibilities available to you in return for offering your gifts to the world, are considerably more than simply cash in exchange for time and skill. Coming into alignment with divine intention is to allow yourself to experience physical, emotional, mental and spiritual abundance, completion, satisfaction and fulfilment.

This planet is intended to be a place of *Shalom* for all beings, not only for humanity. Choosing to experience *Shalom* implicitly means humbly accepting your place in the larger scheme of things, in relation to the environment as a whole, as well as to other people.

---
15 Strong's Concordance 7965 Quoted online at http://www.therefinersfire.org/meaning_of_shalom.htm

Shalom Reduces Difficulties

An aspect of *Shalom* that I encourage you to experience for yourself is allowing life to be easy and flowing.

Not long ago my eldest son was married and Robert and I were taking care of our 18-month-old grandson for two days during and after the wedding. It's a long time since we have had sole charge of an 18-month-old child, and I was anxious about a number of things, including putting up and taking down his stroller, and getting him in and out of the car. In the days leading up to the wedding, I found myself becoming tense and anxious, slipping into an old pattern of focusing on potential difficulties during the time ahead.

Once I noticed that I was putting my energy into imagining problems, I chose to relax and set the intention that the whole experience would be easy and joyful, and that there would always be enough people around to help with whatever needed to be done.

Whenever I found myself becoming tense again, trying to sort things from my human perspective, I chose once again to relax and reaffirmed my choice of ease and flow. Despite my occasional lapses into worry, my overall intention was honoured. The wedding was delightful and the things that I had worried about either didn't happen, or were much more easily managed than I had feared.

Being in alignment with the flow of divine life reduces unnecessary difficulties, hindrance and delays. Let yourself experience *Shalom*.

Your *Shalom* is Unique

You are unique, with a unique spiritual, mental, emotional and physical make-up. The precise nature of your *Shalom* will vary according to your nature, and at different stages in your life.

For me, peace and silence has always been very important. At this point in my life, living in a quiet and secluded place, surrounded by trees, flowers and birds, with lots of physical quiet and time alone, is essential to my well-being and my happiness. It is a central part of my personal *Shalom*.

For someone else, living here would be far too quiet and boring. Be open to discovering what your own unique state of *Shalom* will include.

Main Points of This Chapter
- Life is not meant to be a struggle – the divine intention is for all humanity to experience the state of *Shalom*.
- *Shalom* describes a state of complete well-being, including health, happiness and financial prosperity.
- The quality of life you experience depends upon the choices that you make.
- Being in alignment with the flow of the Life Force reduces unnecessary difficulties, hindrance and delays.

What This Means for Your Business
In implementing the practices in the first part of this section: nurturing a personal relationship with the Life Force through meditation and prayer, healing your trust in the universe, asking for guidance and choosing to be of service by making your unique contribution to the world, you are creating the conditions that will enable you to experience far more prosperity, success, fulfilment and happiness than you have ever imagined.

Wherever you are right now, make the decision to claim your *Shalom*. Make it your personal ambition to open up to the fullness of blessing and prosperity that the universe wants you to experience. If it all possible, speak it out loud. Your unconscious mind will hear and start to act upon it. By choosing to thrive and flourish in every aspect of life, you choose to come into full alignment with who you are designed to be, and become open to the full flow of the Life Force through you, to create what it is that you are here to create. It is a decision that will turbo-boost the growth of your business and every aspect of your life.

When you are in true alignment with who you are, you not only *experience* great joy and fulfilment, but also *become* the great blessing to others that you are intended to be.

You don't have to know how this will happen – you just have to choose to remain open and responsive to your guidance.

Grow Your Business Action Steps
1. Review the other chapters in this section which give you foundational practices for developing your business in partnership with Spirit. If you haven't already done so, choose at least one practice and make it a regular part of your daily schedule.
2. Go to www.JasmineSampson.com/bookresources Download the MP3 of the *Shalom* meditation below and schedule time to listen to it at least once a week.

Meditation: Getting in Touch with Your Shalom

I created this guided visualisation below to help you get in touch with your own unique experience of *Shalom*. This meditation will help you embed your own unique vibration of *Shalom* into the neural networks of your entire body.

If you haven't meditated before, refer to the instructions about meditation on page 28.

Begin as usual with an upright posture, allowing your hands to lie open in your lap. Breathe and relax, letting any distractions or worries flow out with your breath.

As you breathe and relax, bring your attention down – into your hips, your legs, your feet and into the earth. Connect again with the light and love at your sacred centre.

Begin to repeat 'Shalom' as a mantra quietly to yourself. Co-ordinate it with your breath, repeating 'Sha' as you breathe in, and 'lom' as you breathe out. Keep repeating 'Shalom', while you do the visualisations that follow.

Focus all of your attention into your heart, and repeat 'Shalom' into it. Feel the vibration of 'Shalom' in your heart and allow a colour to form. Ask your heart brain to multiply the intensity of the feeling and the colour of your 'Shalom' five times or more.

When this feels complete, on the next out-breath, flow the feeling and the colour of 'Shalom' up into your head. Put all of your attention there and keep repeating 'Shalom' into your head brain. Imagine this frequency flowing through all of your neural pathways, bringing peace, harmony and inspiration to your mental processes.

Allow your awareness of 'Shalom' to include particular aspects that are meaningful for you, such as peace or joy. Ask your head brain to multiply the intensity of its experience of 'Shalom' five times or more.

When this feels complete, flow this expanded experience of 'Shalom' back down to your heart brain. Let yourself feel what it will be like to have all of your heart's deepest desires fulfilled. Multiply and intensify the feeling again. When this feels complete, on the next out-breath gently swallow that magnified feeling down into the gut brain.

Focus 'Shalom' into your gut and allow the gut brain to absorb and multiply the feeling and the colour again. Let yourself feel full, happy, safe and content. When this feels complete, on your next out-breath, flow this multiplied, expanded and intensified awareness of 'Shalom' back to your heart brain.

Keep repeating 'Shalom' into your heart while you allow the light and vibration of your unique 'Shalom' to fill your entire body and the space around you.

Stay resting in the unique vibration of your 'Shalom' for as long as you wish, then gently return your awareness to the everyday world by listening to the sounds around and feeling your feet on the floor.

Stretch and move gently before slowly opening your eyes. You may wish to make a note of your experience in your journal.

Go to www.JasmineSampson.com/bookresources for an MP3 version of this and other meditations

PART II
Growing Your Relationship With Yourself

CHAPTER 10
Embrace Your Uniqueness

Life doesn't have to be a struggle. It becomes a struggle when you think *I should be different* or *the world should be different*. I learned this the slow, hard way.

If you're like me and most of the entrepreneurs I work with, you have big ambitions, huge drive and an enormous amount of energy and motivation to work towards the fulfilment of your dreams. So far so good! But are you also suffering from what I call 'Swan Syndrome?'

Other people see a serene and beautiful creature sailing calmly through life. Underneath, you feel like you are paddling frantically just to stay afloat!

Other people admire you as highly organised, capable, successful and probably good looking as well, and may even be a little in awe of you. Inside you feel like an ugly duckling!

Your instinct is always to see what you haven't done, rather than what you have already achieved. You are very critical of yourself, overlooking your successes and focusing on your mistakes, and are constantly urging yourself to do better.

Do you spend a lot of energy thinking you should be different from the way you are? Do you secretly compare yourself to other, more successful (you think) entrepreneurs and think something like *'S/he's so organised/disciplined/focused/ fill in your own blank! If I only would…then I could be….'*

In other words, do you think you need to *be different in order to be okay and to succeed?* This is one of the big traps of the ego-mind and seems to be almost universally true of the entrepreneurial psyche.

The focus of this chapter is to encourage you to ease up on yourself, embrace your uniqueness and allow your destiny to emerge gently and easily as you stay centred in Spirit. Your destiny is inside you, remember. It will express itself. The question is whether you want to work *with* your impetus for growth, or *against* it.

Let Go of Criticism
In order to fully thrive, it is necessary to surrender your judgements about yourself and about life. Many people resist this, fearing that letting go of their judgements and struggle for change will mean they resign themselves to settle for 'less than the best'. They believe that criticism is necessary to create the motivation for change. The opposite is true. We are designed for growth. When we feel loved and accepted, we naturally expand our boundaries and evolve into new possibilities. Feeling criticised and blamed, on the other hand, shuts us down, and makes us fearful and unwilling to take risks or make mistakes. It doesn't matter whether other people are criticising you, or you are criticising yourself – the effect is the same.

I have found that when I come from the place of totally accepting and loving myself and my life *as it is right now*, that I've liberated energy for new creation. Rejection and judgement of yourself, other people, events, the world and the universe creates an insecure foundation. It is necessary to love and accept yourself totally before you can make lasting changes.

Let Go of Comparisons
One of the tyrannies of the ego-mind is comparing yourself unfavourably with other people, or with preconceived definitions of success. You know the sort of thing: *If I were thinner/stronger/ making more money/married/ single/had children/had no responsibilities/fill in your own blank, then I would be happy and successful.*

In order to fulfil your potential, you need to surrender to your destiny and accept yourself and your life as they are.

Letting Go is Not Giving Up
Surrender doesn't mean giving up, it means letting go. Surrendering to your destiny means letting go of preconceived ideas of who you should be, or how your business should be developing.

It means letting go of trying to organise your life from the level of your one pixel mind, and allowing your life to emerge naturally from the deeper wisdom of the soul. It is here, at the level of your spiritual DNA, that your destiny is written.

This wisdom is within every cell of your being and is expressing itself anyway, whether you like it or not. Your fundamental choice is whether you allow yourself to flow with it and become the best that you can be, or struggle against it and make life unnecessarily difficult for yourself.

Eventually, you will find your way back home to yourself. The question is: do you want to take the quick and easy path, or the long and hard route?

Letting Go of Struggle

Perhaps because gardening is a hobby that I have acquired later in life, I am particularly blessed by all the lessons that I continue to learn from my garden, and which underlie many of the principles I teach in this book.

Just as an acorn comes ready to become an oak tree, provided certain conditions are met that sustain its growth, so there is something innate within you that wants to express itself. An acorn doesn't struggle to become an oak tree. It simply responds to the urgings of its DNA, accepts both the sunshine and the rain, puts down deep roots and allows itself to grow.

You have probably observed that children do much the same thing. It's only as adults that we make life complicated for ourselves.

Let's think about the oak tree further. It does not waste its energy yearning to be a beech tree. It doesn't worry that it doesn't bear fruit like an orange. Nor does it bother comparing itself to other oaks. Our little seedling wastes no time whatsoever wondering about how long it will live or how big it will grow. It puts its energy into growing deep roots to hold on during the winter storms and trusts the Life Force to sustain it. And if it should succumb to storm or drought after a few years, then it is content to allow its body to return to the earth and be reborn as something else.

Accepting Your Place in the Universe

In the economy of my garden, every plant plays its part in the creation of the whole. The humble grass, that is usually only noticed in its absence, is just as important as the biggest tree. The smallest and shyest groundcover that fills up gaps between the larger plants, plays as much part in the beauty of the whole garden as the showiest poppy or rose.

I love the fact that each species of plant is different. Some are annuals, lasting only one season, whilst others live for two years, or five, or 20 and longer. No plant turns round and says: 'I am so ashamed that I'm only an annual. I'm not nearly as good as that tree over there.'

And the most important parts of the garden, essential to the health of all plants, are insects and the invisible microbes in the soil. Without them, nothing would grow.

The lesson: *It's not how visible you are to the world around you that matters in the big scheme of things. It's how well you fulfil your particular role in the unfolding of the universe.*

Become Humble and 'Perfect'

Jesus told his disciples to 'Be perfect, as God in heaven is perfect.'[16] The concept of perfection he was referring to is not some abstract ideal removed from this earth. Perfection in this context refers to how well something fulfils the task for which it was designed. He was telling his followers to do the task they were put on earth to do.

A perfect strawberry plant is one that bears lots of sweet and nourishing fruit, not the one that looks prettiest. If you have ever eaten strawberries grown in an organic garden, you will know that they are infinitely sweeter than their commercially grown counterparts, even if they may not be as big or as regularly shaped.

The English word *humility* has its linguistic root in the Latin word *humus* which means *earth*. Modern English uses *humus* to identify a particular type of soil. For a gardener, humus is the most valuable earth of all. Humus is perfect soil: it is easy to garden, and produces strong, healthy plants.

There is a pride and dignity in accepting your true nature. However big or small your place may be from a human perspective, you are essential to the unfolding of the cosmos. Choosing to focus on making your unique contribution within the divine plan here on earth frees you from false comparisons with anyone else, and allows you to put your energy into being the best 'you' that you can be. This is enormous freedom. Being willing to take your place gives you the dignity of humility, and moves you towards the perfection of which Jesus spoke.

---

16 Matthew 5: 48

When we discussed the concept of *Shalom*, we discovered that the desire of Spirit is to bless you. I have a hunch that the degree to which we accept our place in the unfolding of the universe, and become 'perfect' in the sense I have described it, is the degree to which blessing can flow into our lives.

A foundational step to Growing Business with Soul is to let go of all the expectations you have placed on yourself, or had placed on you by other people, about what you should do, or how you should be.

Start by taking on board the fundamental truths that you are exactly as you should be: that your life has meaning and purpose; that you are here with something special to achieve; that you bring something unique that the world needs. There is a match between your gifts and the world's need, and the universe is designed to support you when you commit to offering your unique package to the world. When you dedicate your life to give of your uniqueness, the universe will step forward to match your commitment.

Do not worry about whether your contribution is big or little, visible or invisible in the human realm. That is not your affair. Your job is to be the best *you* that you can be.

You are a unique expression of divine love. You have a unique vibration, a unique frequency of love, that you bring to everything you are and everything you do. It's not so much *what* you do, as how *you* do it, the intention and attention that *you* bring, that makes *your* unique difference.

When you open yourself fully to allow love to flow through you, and hand over your ego-mind's perceptions of what you should be doing and achieving, then you allow yourself both to *be the blessing* you are designed to be, and to *receive the blessing* that is yours by divine right.

Commit to what you are here to offer, even though you may not know what that is. Continue just as you are. Flourish where you are planted. Assume that you are in exactly the right place, and doing the right things, until you notice that a change is required. Be open to guidance on a daily basis and allow the great wisdom that is inside you to lead the way.

When you see even the smallest and most mundane activities of life as part of your offering to the well-being of the whole, life takes on a sacred dimension which brings great joy. When you fully embrace as a sacred contract who you are, and what you are here to do and be, then life becomes magic. There is a satisfaction and fulfilment in surrendering to who you are designed to be that nothing else will bring you.

Celebrate Slow Growth

Western culture teaches us to value things that happen fast. We are trained to expect quick results and become discouraged and critical if they do not appear. This is not the way of nature. Mushrooms may come up overnight, but they disappear just as fast.

A wise woman once said to me 'trees and people grow slowly'. In most cases, the slower the growth of the tree, the stronger the wood. So it is with people. If you are a slow developer, then celebrate. Think of yourself as being like the palm trees that survive tornadoes. They can spend eight to fourteen years putting down their roots before ever a frond appears above soil. Once they begin to shoot, they come up quickly, but their strength and ability to survive hurricane-force gales comes from the time and energy they put into growing those roots.

Time and patience are needed to come to maturity and bear fruit. You are a work in progress. Give yourself the gift of time and patience. Let yourself grow slowly, be patient and focus on enjoying each day to its fullest and bringing the fullness of you to everything you do.

Once again, let go of your expectations of how you should be, or what results you should see, or when. Surrender to the destiny inscribed on your DNA and let Spirit worry about what happens next. Celebrate your progress and allow the business you are destined to create to grow through you.

Main Points of This Chapter

- You are designed for growth.
- It is necessary to love and accept yourself totally before you can make lasting changes.
- Embrace your destiny and accept yourself and your life as they are in order to fulfil your potential.
- However big or small your place may be from a human perspective, you are essential to the unfolding of the cosmos.

What this Means for Your Business

Take an honest look at your business plans and goals. Are these derived from the ego-mind or from your soul? Let go of how big you think your business should be at any particular stage of development and focus on:

a) Growing yourself and your consciousness
b) Appreciating what you have already created
c) Bringing the very best 'you' to everything you do right now

Grow Your Business Action Steps

1. Review Chapter 4 (Prayer) and 6 (Global Jigsaw). Commit to doing the work you are here to do and give thanks that Spirit is guiding and blessing you
2. Do the *Shalom* meditation each week

Go to www.JasmineSampson.com/bookresources for resources for this chapter.

CHAPTER 11
Practise Forgiveness

Forgiveness is ... our passport to divine greatness while we're still engrossed in the experience of our humanity. –Dannion Brinkley[17]

As an expression of the Life Force, human beings are meant to be free-flowing like a wave or a river. Unprocessed events, judgements, negative emotions, and other mental and emotional 'debris' slow down and reduce the flow of the life force within us. Instead of being light, sparkling and free, and able to respond joyfully to every subtle movement of energy, the life force of most people becomes dull and sluggish. Life becomes a struggle and often sadness and sickness result.

Every life has stuff that hurts. We have all done things that we regret. We have not done things that we wish we had. Other people have hurt us, intentionally and unintentionally. And we are born into families, cultures, and a world families, cultures and a world with a huge history of suffering. The pains of the past continue to reverberate until they are released and healed. It is part of your soul purpose to help relieve the suffering of the world in your own special way. You are here to transform your own life, and in so doing, you help transform the lives of other people.

Forgiveness is a process that begins with the *choice* to let go of pain and that takes as long as it takes. Some hurts are dealt with in a few moments. Others can take weeks, months or even years to completely heal. I find it helpful to keep affirming my ongoing choice to let go and forgive at each stage of the healing journey.

---

17   *Secrets of the Light* p.44

Understanding Forgiveness

In my experience, forgiveness is often misunderstood. Many people think that forgiving is excusing unacceptable behaviour, or saying that what happened doesn't matter. Others think that forgiveness cannot be extended until the other person has expressed regret for what they have done. Still others refuse to forgive because they think the other person deserves to be punished for what they have done. Or that choosing to forgive is something you do for the other person. None of this is true.

Forgiveness is first and foremost something that you do for yourself. When you choose to forgive, you give yourself the gift of freeing up the life energy that's within you, releasing you from being burdened by memories of what has gone before. Forgiveness is letting go of the past so that you can be free to move forward into a happier future. The feelings of release and healing *follow* the choice to let go and forgive. Sometimes this happens instantly. Often it takes time and repeated choosing of the decision to forgive to complete the healing process.

Refusing to forgive keeps you chained to painful memories and trapped in the past. Lack of forgiveness restricts the flow of Life Force within you. Research clearly shows that bitterness creates toxic chemicals in the body which undermine physical health. Refusing to forgive is like swallowing poison and hoping the other person will become ill.

In this life, some pain is inevitable. However, suffering is optional. Suffering occurs when we resist what is, and when we hold on to the pain of the past. Forgiveness, or letting go, is a foundational practice for bringing healing to ourselves and the situations around us. Choosing to forgive takes our past pain and mistakes, and enables them to become a resource that nourishes us now and a strength that we can offer to others. We teach best what we have struggled to learn ourselves.

If you are serious about transforming your life and fulfilling your potential, get serious about forgiveness. Forgiveness is an essential practice for health of every kind – mental, emotional and physical. Choosing to forgive yourself and other people on a daily basis is one of the most empowering choices you can make.

Forgiving is not …

- Trying to forget, pretending it didn't happen
- Something to be withheld until the other person says *sorry*
- Getting back, getting over, getting even
- Saying it doesn't matter
- Smothering the conflict
- Excusing the other person
- Tolerating
- Pardoning
- Seeking reconciliation
- A feeling
- Easy
- Cheap

Forgiving is …

- A decision – not to continue holding a burden of pain any longer
- A choice
- More of a journey than a destination
- A process that takes time
- Part of self-healing
- Refusing to remain a victim
- Learning to love and to live
- Something you do for yourself more than for the other person
- Refusing to allow the pain of the past to continue to cripple you
- A vital spiritual and emotional practice with profound results for yourself and others

Forgiveness Begins with a Choice

Most often life presents little stuff that we can let go of relatively easily. But when something is huge and the damage extensive – the 'unforgiveable' things we encounter – we dare not wait until we *feel* ready to let go. That time will never come. Make the *choice* to let go – and the feelings will follow as you stay faithful to your process. I share the following with you, not only because it is such a powerful example of the healing power of forgiveness, but also because it demonstrates clearly how healing of emotions *follow the choice to forgive*.

Forgiveness Transforms

During my time as a hospital chaplain, I was privileged to work closely with a young woman I will call Alison, who had been severely sexually abused from childhood through to her adolescence. The scars of this ongoing abuse ran very deep and Alison had a significant psychiatric disorder. We bonded deeply and worked together closely over a period of several years, both during my time at the hospital and after I left.

At one point Alison was part of an extended workshop I was running, of which one of the modules was focused on forgiveness, and I gave participants the same *Forgiveness Process* that I give you later in this chapter.

Alison chose to forgive her abuser and asked me to help her in what for her was an extremely difficult process. She was trembling and sweating as we went into the meditation. Each time I asked her if she was sure she was ready to continue, she said *yes*, and so we completed the process of confronting the abusive image that she carried around inside her, and brought release to her memories.

She said to me afterwards that, as we began the process, there was an enormous pain around her heart, rather like a solid brick wall that extended as far as she could see. As she came to the words of forgiveness, this pain and pressure intensified and it was only her willpower that enabled her to continue.

As soon as she spoke the words of the *Releasing Prayer*, the pain and the wall around her heart completely dissolved, and were replaced with a warmth and peace that she had never before experienced. More than ten years later I can still remember how radiant she looked.

Her journey continued to have twists and turns and challenges of various types, but this first step of forgiveness marked a turning point in her journey of healing, and she never again visited the depths of despair that she had once experienced so regularly.

Forgive Yourself

As I said in the last chapter, in my experience all entrepreneurs have very high standards and constantly beat themselves up for even minor mistakes. Learning to forgive yourself is even more important for your growth and wellbeing than forgiving others. If there are things in your past that you are not at peace about, you can use these steps to deal with them.

Set aside 30 minutes to make an honest list of what needs attention. Many people (including me) are more bothered by the good we have not done, than by active wrongs we have done.

1. For each item on the list ask what (if anything) you need to do to correct the situation.
2. Do what you can to put things right.

Go to www.JasmineSampson.com/bookresources and use the *Forgive Yourself* Tapping video listed for this chapter.

Undertake to pray regularly for other people affected by your action (or lack of action). When you think of them simply say (out loud or silently) *I send a blessing of love, healing and peace to …* Do this every time they come to mind.

Healing Processes

Every human being needs tools for emotional healing. Here's why:

An important part of our limbic brain, or emotional brain, is the amygdala which is focused on maintaining our physical survival. Our ancestors had two options: to think there was a dangerous animal hiding in that bush, when there wasn't, or to think that there was nothing dangerous in that bush, when there was. In terms of pure physical survival, it was a better strategy to assume that danger lurked everywhere, and so humans are hardwired to remember the unpleasant and dangerous experiences of our lives, and overlook the pleasant and happy ones.

The amygdala is constantly scanning our surroundings for real or imagined threats to our safety. When the amygdala perceives a threat, it releases adrenaline. This prepares us physically to fight the perceived danger, run away from it, or if neither of these is possible, to freeze. Most of the anxieties and threats we face today are not physical. We can't run away from an unexpected tax-bill, for example. When there is no physical way to create safety, the stressful event becomes frozen in our cells and neural pathways.

Every time we encounter a situation that *the emotional brain thinks is similar to the original event*, the amygdala releases the same flood of stress hormones and our negative emotions are activated. That is why we sometimes find ourselves upset in ways that seem totally out of proportion to the incident that triggered it.

Your emotional brains evolved several million years before the part of your brain that deals with language. Telling yourself *it's silly to feel this way* does not work. **Your emotions do not understand words; they need experience in order to heal.**

I use a number of healing processes personally and with clients. Here are two that I recommend you learn and incorporate into your personal growth toolkit. You can join me in video demonstrations and download full instructions for these processes at www.JasmineSampson.com/bookresources

1. **Focusing** is gentle way of connecting with the healing and wisdom contained in your body, and involves bringing compassionate awareness to where you are holding pain or tension. Being aware of your body's response to a situation is a foundational skill that is transformational in its own right. I also use this process as part of Tapping and other healing processes.
2. **Tapping**, also known as Emotional Freedom Technique or EFT. This technique can be useful in just about any situation, to both clear negative emotions and anchor positive choices. It rewires the brain to release painful memories and evokes the body's relaxation response. I use it daily as a part of my self-care and meditation practice.

I highly recommend that you join me as I guide you through Focusing and the other healing processes I refer to in this chapter at www.JasmineSampson.com/bookresources

A Process to Release Past Pain
Stage 1: Identify What Still Hurts

I suggest that you start a Healing Journal to record what needs working on. You will gain valuable insights into your inner life this way.

Start by setting aside 60 minutes when you won't be disturbed to do a life survey. State your intention to heal the major hurts of your past and ask that the things that need attention will be brought to mind.

Work through your life decade by decade and write down any memory that causes tension in your body, or a feeling of unhappiness or discomfort when you think about it. Rate the intensity of your discomfort out of 10, with 10 being highest. Add to the list as more things come to mind.

Starting with the things that have the highest rating, work through your list systematically until you are clear. Many people choose to do one per day until they are done.

If it is a traumatic event that you are focusing on for the first time, you may need to spend some time allowing the pain and hurt to the surface first. *If you need support during this process make sure that you get it.*

It is extremely important that you listen to your own pain first. Your story needs to be heard and fully appreciated on the journey towards wholeness and life. It may be necessary for you to spend some time expressing your anger, rage and pain before you are ready to let go fully. Regard this as part of the forgiveness process.

In listening to the pain of your younger self, bring gentle observation and compassionate acceptance to your experience. Focusing, which I mentioned above, will teach you how to gently acknowledge your thoughts, body sensations and emotions as they arise, without becoming overwhelmed.

Here are some suggestions about ways to allow the pain to come to the surface. Remember that the focus of all these processes is *healing and release* – watch for the part of you that may want to feed, hold onto or magnify your hurt and anger. To avoid getting stuck in the pain, I suggest that you affirm out loud your intention to heal at the beginning and end of the process and at any stage when the pain becomes intense.

I regularly affirm *I am willing to let this go* when I am dealing with painful emotions.

- **Write a letter you aren't going to send.** Say exactly what you want to all the other people involved. Be as angry as you need to be, and don't mind your language or your spelling. When I do this, I find that I often come through to a place of release where I am able to express some degree of forgiveness, but don't force this. That step can come later, for now you need to honour your own story. When you are finished, **put the letter aside for a time – then burn it** within a few hours, or next day
- **Draw or scribble** using the hand you don't normally write with to liberate 'stuck' emotions. This is especially helpful if you were very young at the time of the painful event – before the age of 4 or 5. Allow your subconscious mind to express itself freely and keep writing/drawing even if it seems like nonsense. Be compassionate with what comes up from this young part of yourself.

Stage 2: Release the Experience

The quickest and most powerful method of releasing and healing the past is undoubtedly Tapping which has been shown to be particularly effective in releasing traumatic memories and creating new neural pathways, literally rewiring the brain.

I tap through the points, while letting myself feel what hurts, without judging myself, until I feel release. Whilst I am tapping I use phrases such as: *I choose to love and accept myself*; *I am willing to let this go*; and *I invite Love to heal this pain*. You will undoubtedly find the words that work well for you.

Alternatively, try imagining the situation as if you were watching a video. Press pause when you wish and go and rescue the younger self. Sit the younger 'you' on your lap and talk together about what happened. Focus on accepting your inner child's pain and anger, offering comfort and reassurance that you are there for her/him now. The stored pain will dissolve of its own accord as you offer your unconditional acceptance and support.

Stage 3: Forgiveness Meditation
Once you have brought some initial healing to your feelings about what happened, you may wish to move onto the *Forgiveness Meditation* straight away, or you may wish to wait until later.

The following *Forgiveness Meditation* is exceptionally powerful and you will find it useful for the major things that need healing both in your past, present and future. Healing of any sort is very much a clearing out process, and I recommend you end every healing session by inviting love and/or white light to fill all the places which have been accessed in your process.

Download an MP3 version of the following meditation at www.JasmineSampson.com/bookresources

Forgiveness Meditation
This meditation is a three step process. It is important to allow yourself the time you need to heal fully. Stop at the end of any section if you do not feel ready to proceed. Return to the process as often as you need for deep healing.

Part 1
Sit or lie comfortably and take some deep breaths, letting go of tension and anxiety as you breathe out. Breathe your awareness down into the earth and allow yourself to be filled with the love and peace of the golden light in your sacred place.

Imagine yourself breathing in gold and white light and healing love with each breath. Allow the light to wash over you and fill you, dissolving fear, regret and pain. Allow the light to fill you and experience the warmth of Unconditional Love filling you from the inside out, like a warm glowing fire of peace. See yourself encased in an egg of light.

Repeat a prayer of blessing to yourself – say it out loud for preference.

Use these words or others that are meaningful to you:

> I open myself to release the pain of my past
> May Love and Healing flow
> through my past, my present, and my future
> to bring transformation and peace.

Rest in the love and light and peace, allowing it to flow into you and to touch and heal all hurt and tensions. Do not rush this part. Take plenty of time for your own healing. You may wish to end your meditation time here and return to the process at another time.

Part 2

When you are ready, gently allow the thought of the other person to come to you. Take note of what happens in your body when you think of this person. Ask healing love and light to wash away any tension or hurt as it appears.

You may wish to end your meditation time here and return to the process at another time.

Part 3

When you are ready, allow this person to appear in front of you. Concentrate on the feeling of peace and love and light filling you. Ask healing love and light to fill you both and dissolve all hurt.

When you feel ready, imagine love and light surrounding and filling this person. Stay like this for as long as it feels appropriate. If you wish, you may repeat a blessing or prayer for them.

Use these words or others that appeal to you:

> I release you to Spirit
> I pray blessing upon you
> I pray that you will be fulfilled and happy and guided to your Highest Good.
> I ask for the very best for you.

Stay with the awareness of light and love filling the other person, until you feel ready to allow them to fade gently from your awareness.

Finish the process by praying for yourself. You can use these words or others that feel appropriate to you:

> And as I release you to your Highest Good, so I ask for the very best for me.
>
> I put my life in Divine hands
>
> I choose for my heart to be healed
>
> I choose to become full of peace and joy
>
> I choose to be guided and prospered
>
> I choose to fulfil my Soul Purpose
>
> I choose to receive my Highest Good.
>
> And I give thanks that this is so.

Pray this prayer with real intention. You will have a sense of release when you do so.

Afterwards

Whenever you think of the person or situation, simply repeat aloud an affirmation or prayer. Here are some suggestions you may like to use, or you can write your own:

- *I give thanks that the Highest Good is being done*
- *Only good will come of this*
- *Divine Love is doing a perfect work and all is well*
- *I open my heart to receive blessing and joy*

Forgiveness Is a Lifetime Practice

You will never be done with this life-giving practice. I believe that when we choose to work deeply with the discipline of forgiveness, we are bringing healing not only to ourselves but also to our ancestors, and the communities of which we are a part. Depending on your cultural roots, you will have greater or lesser amounts of inherited betrayals, slights, hurts and tragedies to deal with.

After a lifetime of practising forgiveness, I have recently discovered bitterness and a desire for revenge buried deep within my gut. You see, I have Scots ancestry, and I recognise that bitterness and revenge are part of my spiritual DNA. It echoes subtly down my family tree. Choosing to love, accept and release these bitter and resentful parts of my ancestral heritage has been an important part of my ongoing choice to let go of past pain and all of its crippling effects, not only for me but for everyone connected to me.

Wherever you are in the journey of forgiveness, be gentle with yourself. Approach your particular story with compassion and gentleness and understand that every time you choose to let go of pain and bitterness, you are freeing up the Life Force to flow more strongly within you. It will bring healing and freedom to you and everyone with whom you are involved.

Main Points of This Chapter
- Forgiveness is a gift we make to ourselves.
- It begins with a choice to be free of past pain.
- It is a process that may take a long time.
- Feelings follow the choice to forgive.
- Forgiving yourself is as important as forgiving others.
- We are hardwired to remember the unpleasant and dangerous experiences of our lives.
- Our emotions need experience in order to heal.

What This Means for Your Business
Unresolved pain and regret from your past saps the energy and drive you need for living now. The longer it remains buried the more toxic it becomes. Realise that every part of your life, including your business, suffers as a result and make it a priority to release this now. If you need help and support, get it.

Grow Your Business Action Steps
1. Use the processes outlined in this chapter to clear past issues that need healing.
2. Learn the skills of Focusing and Tapping to help you process difficult emotions as they arise. (I coach you through both of these at www.JasmineSampson.com/bookresources)
3. Keep yourself clear by staying tuned to your inner responses as you go about your day. Pay attention when pain and discomfort come up and note whether the discomfort is physical or emotional. In particular, stay alert for signals from your heart and your gut, as they will give you valuable information about what is happening in your inner world. The faster you can process the information your body and emotions give you, the quicker you will grow.

Find more resources at www.JasmineSampson.com/bookresources

PART III
Growing Your Relationship with Other People

CHAPTER 12
Let Go of Judgement

The essence of spiritual growth and healing is restoring our vision of ourselves and of the world to wholeness: shifting our perception from fragmentation to unity; from seeing life as a series of haphazard events, to perceiving the underlying unity of all things. In spiritual terms this is often called developing a unitive consciousness, or a heart-centred perspective. Jesus referred to it as 'seeing with a single eye'.[18]

As we have seen, the research of quantum scientists is confirming what spiritual writers have told us for centuries – that everything in the universe is connected at an invisible level. When the world is a series of connections, judgement separates and divides things that in essence are joined. When I decide that you are wrong and I am right, I close a door in my heart that ultimately shuts us both out of the place of truth where true healing and restoration can occur.

Equally, when I reject a part of myself that I don't like or don't approve of, the results are just as destructive. As one woman said to me when describing her inner resistance to letting go of her judgment: 'I've created a barbed wire fence inside. And I see that the barbs point in both directions.'

Judgement or Discernment?
A few years ago, I was posed a question that set me thinking deeply. I was leading a *Relationship Healing Retreat*, and we'd done some processes to clear ourselves of the accumulated guilt and shame and blame that leaks out to poison our closest relationships.

---
[18] Mark 9:47

A young woman raised the question: 'It's all very well to clear my guilt and self-judgement, but what if I *have* behaved badly? What if I could have done things better? What about taking responsibility for *my* part in the breakdown of the friendship?'

It was a terrific question and it touches so deeply into the heart of our human experience that I want to explore it a little here.

She was referring, I believe, to two different responses which in English are often lumped together under the one word: *judgement*. 'I judge that you have committed a crime' and 'I judge that this is the best course of action to take'.

While the same word *judge* is used in both these instances, they refer to two very different inner processes, and I will use the words *judgement* and *discernment* to clarify the difference. In essence, the energy of judgement closes doors, whereas discernment finds a path.

Experiencing Judgement
When I respond to something or someone in judgement, it feels like a door closing in my chest. To feel it for yourself, try this exercise.

Spend a few minutes thinking about something that makes you feel open and loving – a little child, a favourite pet, even a beautiful landscape. Notice how relaxed and light you feel in your chest and around your heart.

Now think about something you did that you regret or are ashamed of. You will probably notice a shift in your chest.

That feeling of tightness means you are judging yourself. You have shut out a part of yourself – and that part will continue to hurt and to play out in unexpected ways in your life, until it is allowed back into your consciousness and re-integrated into your being.

Because everything is joined, it doesn't matter whether I am closing my heart to you or to part of me – both create division and pain. Ultimately, both actions are less than the highest possibility for ourselves and for others.

The Price of Holding on to Judgement
In terms of energy, this form of judgement really does limit the amount of love and joy you can experience in your life. That is why bitterness leads ultimately to sickness. Close your heart often enough in the course of a lifetime and you literally shut off the supply of Life Force in your system.

You quite simply close down the body's ability to renew itself and heal. Ignoring your inner voice also closes the heart and creates distrust between different aspects of yourself. Do it often enough and a deep underlying sadness, and often sickness, will result.

The good news is that this process can be reversed. When you decide to let go, to open the door again, then Life Force automatically rushes back in to fill the part that was closed. That is why every spiritual tradition stresses the need to forgive others and forgive ourselves.

If judgement is not the best way to navigate our way through the world, how then are we to make decisions or decide on a course of action? There are choices that are destructive and cause pain for ourselves and others. How are we to respond to these?

Cultivating Discernment

That is where discernment comes in. Discernment feels very different. Discernment comes more from the heart than the rational mind. It is intuitive rather than logical, has a grasp on the big picture of life that is hidden to the ego-mind, and is able to respond to subtle shifts and movements in a situation.

Judgement (in the sense I am referring to it) tends to make one decision and stick with it. Discernment can recognise that today is a new day and that yesterday's decision may need to be adjusted subtly to fit today's circumstances.

Judgement sits down with an old map to try to plan a way into tomorrow. Discernment reads the signs, sees that the sands have shifted and that the best route to where we want to go has moved.

Discernment can choose the path of highest possibility for ourselves and others, without closing energetically against the paths not chosen. It says, *I choose this* and simply turns attention in that direction. Remaining open and free, discernment does not need to justify itself, nor push against another choice.

Judgement by its very nature is closed and rigid. Discernment remains alive and fluid and open. Judgement keeps our ego self (the self that believes in separation) in control. Discernment requires that we walk forward in trust, that we learn from our mistakes, and that we keep growing and expanding in our awareness and our understanding. Judgement is based on yesterday's experience. Discernment is operating out of the here and now.

The Result of Choosing Discernment

So, coming back to the question asked at the retreat, the answer lies in choosing discernment over judgement so that we can clear the baggage of conscious and unconscious judgements. These are judgements about ourselves and others which restrict the flow of life and love and joy in any of our relationships. And once that is gone – once we can see everyone, including ourselves, clearly and with compassion – then we are in a place to discern where our actions need to be changed, where an apology is owing or when we need to speak up about something that is troubling us.

When we clear the accumulated poison from our unconscious minds, then what we need to do and say can be done freely and openly – without the hidden agendas which cause such friction and unhappiness. And when we are free and open, it is amazing how free and open others become in response.

If you think you may be holding onto judgement, review and use the Healing Processes in Chapter 11.

How Do I Let Go of Judgement?

This is a good time to introduce another of my favourite healing processes. Z Point (created by Canadian Grant Connolly of www.ZPointforpeace.com) is a fantastic 'Power Shovel' method to quickly clear an entire situation by gathering all the negative emotions connected to a situation and releasing them together.

Joanne was extremely angry and distressed by the behaviour of her step-daughter, whom I shall call Tanya. The girl was aged about twelve and behaving in a number of ways that were destructive for the peace and well-being of the family. Being caught in the dynamics of the step-parenting relationship made the situation even more difficult for Joanne and she came to me for help.

At the beginning of our session she rated her anger and dislike whenever she thought of Tanya as 10/10. I guided her through a 45-minute Z Point meditation process, during which she progressively released deeper and deeper layers of negative emotions and unconscious judgements about this situation and others like it. At the end of our time, she was amazed and delighted to discover that she now felt peaceful and calm when she thought of Tanya.

Three days later, she rang me in great excitement to say that the family had experienced their happiest weekend ever. She described Tanya as being calm, polite and co-operative – 'like a totally different person'.

By clearing out her own conscious and unconscious negative judgements Joanne had enabled an entirely new relationship dynamic to form within the family.

Main Points of This Chapter
- Although we tend to use the same word, judgement and discernment are two different processes.
- Judgement comes from the head, while discernment is an activity of the heart.
- Judgement relies on past experience and closes us down to new possibilities.
- Discernment finds a new path to a new future.
- Releasing conscious and unconscious judgements about other people is a powerful way to create new possibilities.

What This Means for Your Business
Many people will be very clear about their personal relationships, but may accept niggles and irritations as part of life in a business context. Your life is one whole – and how your energy flows in any part of it has a direct connection with how it flows in business.

Unconscious expectations and judgement are a big factor in how other people behave towards us. If you are experiencing difficulties such as unreliable employees, dishonest contractors or bad debts, then first turn your attention inwards to clear your contribution to the relationship. See the activity suggestions below for how to do this.

Clearing out conscious and unconscious judgements in all your relationships will free up the flow of the Life Force, which will enable more opportunities, inspiration and money to come in your direction.

Cultivating the skill of discernment – remaining open-hearted to yourself and other people while making business decisions – will mean that you are consistently open to the highest possibility for all.

Grow Your Business Action Steps

1. Take an inventory of your business relationships. Is there a client/colleague/employee who regularly pushes your buttons? Make a list of the thoughts and emotions you have around them.
2. Then go online to www.JasmineSampson.com/bookresources and work through the Z Point process with me.
3. Practise tuning into your heart when you make decisions. Choose the thing that leaves you feeling peaceful and open-hearted.

Meditation
The Z Point process is the meditation for this chapter.
www.JasmineSampson.com/bookresources

CHAPTER 13
Use the Technology of Love

I don't know if the phrase *Technology of Love* is original to me, but I have begun to use it recently to refer to a conscious and focused use of the power of love to create a significant positive shift in a situation. I find it helpful to realise that just as I use the technology of the internet to send an email, even though I can't see the means by which my message is communicated across the world, so focusing my thoughts with loving intention also uses an invisible technology to create a discernible outcome.

I talked at some length in Chapter 2 about the nature of Love as the fundamental creative power of the universe. Here we look at some specific ways you can use what I call Miracle-Producing Love.

Miracle-Producing Love in Action
Miracle-Producing Love is realistic and honest. It is prepared to acknowledge pain and suffering, but it does so with compassion and forgiveness, rather than judgement. It does this, not to be 'nice', but to be practical. As we have already discussed, judgement locks things into place. Forgiveness enables new possibilities to emerge.

As we learned in Chapter 1, quantum research shows that the stuff which makes up our physical reality is affected by our DNA – and our DNA is affected by our emotions. In other words, *your world is created moment to moment by your emotional response to life.*

If you stay focused on the difficulties you are currently experiencing, or the mistakes you and other people are making, you are locking in place the emotional conditions that will keep the same things happening.

When you are hurt, or find a part of somebody else that you don't like, you have two choices. You can choose to judge and reject them, and close the door of your heart, so keeping the hurt part of yourself trapped. Or you can choose to accept that in the Quantum Field we're all connected, and so, at the invisible level, this person is part of you. When you choose to invite love to heal every aspect of yourself, the other person and the situation, you open a door for powerful transformation in your own life, and the life of everyone connected to you.

A Course in Miracles[19] would say that all human action is either an expression of love or a cry for love. When you choose to look past another person's hurtful and destructive behaviour and focus on the divine spark within them, you are giving them the gift of Miracle-Producing Love. You are also acting from your own divine essence and in accordance with your own true nature of Love.

When you choose to believe in the good at the heart of other people, you hold open the door for them to find the passage to who they could be, rather than who they have been up until now.

Using Love to Shift the Dynamics of a Relationship
To create something new, you need to do three things:

1. Look honestly at what is happening.
2. Process how you feel about it so that you can let go of judgement and allow something new to emerge.
3. Focus on the best-possible outcome. Believe in yourself and believe in other people.

Let's take a look at what this looks like in practice.
Linda is a highly creative woman, who discussed with me her extreme irritation at the mess that her husband Don, left on his side of the bed. Beauty and order are important values for Linda and her sensitive energy was impacted by the clutter of books and papers piled high on the bedside cabinet and on the floor.

She was conflicted between her need for order in her environment, and her desire to respect Don's freedom to be himself in this shared space. Linda's first step was to acknowledge the possibility that her resistance was playing a part in keeping Don's habitual clutter in place.

---

19 *A Course in Miracles*. 1975, 1985. Foundation for Inner Peace.

She identified that she felt this resistance as tightness and tension in her chest and shoulders, and that these were accompanied by feelings of anger and thoughts of: *you just don't care about what is important to me.*

Rather than talking about the problem with Don, which she knew from experience would have little lasting effect, Linda decided to use the *Technology of Love* to bring healing to the part of her that was distressed, and set herself the goal of feeling at peace, regardless of what the floor on Don's side of the bed looked like.

Each day she spent five minutes morning and evening, directing four healing phrases into the tightness and tension she felt in her body about this issue: *I love you. I am sorry. Please forgive me. Thank you.*

As she persevered, she became aware that she was healing deeply buried negative emotions and subtle expectations that had been hidden below her conscious awareness.

After a few weeks of keeping her focus on healing herself, instead of trying to change Don, she reported to me that the mess on his side of her bed no longer drew her eye, and that she was no longer distressed by it. She had achieved her goal and the topic dropped off our conversation list.

I forgot all about it until six months later, when she reported to me that she had suddenly noticed that Don no longer left a mess on his side of the bed. In fact she showed me 'before' and 'after' photos, and it was hard to believe they belonged to the same man!

And all of this happened without saying a word to Don directly. By changing her habitual *emotional* response to the situation, Linda had sent a new message via her DNA into the universal consciousness, and a new reality had formed out of the Quantum Field.

Using the Technology of Love

The *Technology of Love* can be engaged in many ways, from meditation and prayer to something as simple as repeating *love, love, love* to yourself whenever you find a situation or experience that you wish to heal, whether it is in your own life or somebody else's. Any act of kindness, compassion or forgiveness, to yourself and to others, uses the *Technology of Love* and has the capacity to create miracles.

Introducing Ho'oponopono

The process that Linda used in the example above is an ancient Hawaiian practice of reconciliation and forgiveness, known as Ho'oponopono. It is one of my most favourite ways to help myself and my clients release negative emotions and allow Love to heal the heart and change the situation. It combines very well with Tapping and is also part of my 'daily-use' toolkit.

Ho'oponopono recognises that everything is connected and involves four simple statements that work to bring healing to the underlying causes of illness or any other trouble. The statements are:

1. *I love you*
2. *I am sorry*
3. *Please forgive me*
4. *Thank you*

Learn more about Ho'oponopono and how to use it at www.JasmineSampson.com/bookresources

Main Points of This Chapter
- Staying focused on current difficulties keeps them locked in place.
- All human actions are either an expression of love or a call for love.
- Believing in the good at the heart of other people enables them to move towards becoming who they could be instead of who they have been.
- Using the *Technology of Love* is a highly effective way to shift the dynamics of difficult relationships within your business.

What This Means for Your Business

Choosing to use the *Technology of Love* to heal situations around you positions you as a powerful channel of divine action in the world. This is the highest possible calling for any human being.

By releasing the judgements of your limited human ego, you inevitably open up to a high-octane spiritual power flowing into every part of your life, including your business. You plant yourself firmly in the path of blessing, guidance, opportunities and everything else you need to prosper and thrive. It is the pathway to your *Shalom* and to steady expansion into manifesting the very highest possibility for your life and business.

Grow Your Business Action Steps
1. Learn the four Ho'oponopono phrases and use them whenever you experience delay or difficulty in your business affairs.
2. When you encounter negative behaviour in others choose to see it as a cry for love, and choose one of the ways suggested above to respond.
3. Regularly use the *Loving-Kindness* meditation below for everyone connected with your business.

Loving-Kindness Meditation for Your Business
Loving-Kindness meditation has a long history in the Buddhist tradition. It was taught by the Buddha as a practice to 'sweeten the mind and practise selfless love' and can be adapted very easily to fit any framework of belief. Here is a version I have adapted for business.

Start in the usual way – sitting upright, feet flat on the floor and your spine straight.

Take three deep cleansing breaths in through your nose and out through your mouth, remembering to relax your jaw as you breathe out. Consciously relax from the top of your head down through the entire body on the out breath. Imagine you are gathering all your tension together as you breathe in, and then gently releasing it. Breathe your awareness down into the earth and connect again to the light of love.

Gently observe your body as you let your breathing settle into a normal rhythm. Keeping a gentle focus on your breathing, repeat quietly to yourself 'I am filled with peace' *for a few breaths until you feel full of peace.*

Then repeat 'I am filled with forgiveness' *for a few more breaths.*

Finally say 'I am filled with love' *and let the feeling of love arise with you. Imagine love as golden light filling your heart and permeating your whole being. Realise that love is a natural part of you and an intrinsic quality of the true Self. Think of times when you experienced love and joy for yourself, life and others.*

Keep repeating 'love, love, love' *quietly to yourself as a mantra. Begin to feel love and light expanding from you and permeating the room. Allow the light and love to expand out of you and imagine it filling your family with joy and peace. Quietly say to them:* 'May you be blessed with love and peace.'

Allow the light and love to expand to fill all the people associated with the delivery of your business – employees, contractors and others who enable your business to function. Quietly say to them 'May you be blessed with love and peace.'

Expand your circle of golden light and love to include your office and workplace. If you have an internet based business, imagine it flowing into your website and throughout the World Wide Web.

Imagine the golden light of love expanding to include all who benefit from your business – clients and customers, people on your list. Imagine them filled with the beautiful golden light of love, happy and fulfilled. Quietly say to them: 'May you be blessed with love and peace.'

Imagine the golden light of love expanding further to include people you don't yet know who need your business. Imagine them filled with the beautiful golden light of love, happy and fulfilled. Quietly say to them: 'May you be blessed with love and peace.'

Allow your circle of golden light and love to expand to include your town or city. Imagine all people filled with the beautiful golden light of love, happy and fulfilled. Quietly say to them: 'May you be blessed with love and peace.'

Allow your circle of golden light and love to expand to flow throughout your country. Imagine all people filled with the beautiful golden light of love, happy and fulfilled. Quietly say to them: 'May you be blessed with love and peace.'

Allow the light of love to reach out and embrace all countries in the world and then expand out to the whole universe. Mentally say 'May all share in this love.' *Then wish all love, peace and contentment.*

Be still for a while and let love naturally flow out from you, then gently breathe your awareness back up into your surroundings and return to normal consciousness. Take the love you have built with you as you go about your day.

Go to www.JasmineSampson.com/bookresources for an MP3 of this *Loving Kindness* Meditation and other resources for this chapter

PART IV
Growing Your Relationship with the World Around

CHAPTER 14
Ask for More Money

No book on spirituality for entrepreneurs would be complete without a discussion of money. Mentally and emotionally, money can be a difficult topic to embrace. Many people, even entrepreneurs, are very uncomfortable with the idea of asking for more.

One of the consequences of our mistaken belief that lack is a foundational principle in this world, is that we have created a belief that there is only so much money to go around: if I have more, then somebody else is going to have less.

A History of Money

In former times this concept made sense. Money is a means of trade in our society. In earlier times trade was direct: I exchanged my excess apples for your excess eggs and we both profited.

As societies became more complex, and the variety of available goods expanded, traders emerged. Rather than directly exchanging goods and services, middlemen developed, who bought desirable items from others to on-sell at a profit. At this point, the concept of *money* – an agreed object that represented wealth or the ability to offer something of value in exchange for something purchased – developed as a means of indirect exchange.

Over the centuries, in different cultures around the world, *money* has been (and still is) represented by items as varied as shells, engraved ivory cylinders, blankets, muskets, and cows, to name but a few. In our world, *money* is represented physically by small discs of embossed metal and colourful pieces of paper.

As the concept of scarcity developed, things that were difficult to acquire, such as gold and diamonds, came to be perceived as of most value, even though these minerals have never been able to do anything useful, such as feed, clothe, educate or heal a solitary soul! It is actually far more logical to see goats and cows as wealth. These animals contribute ongoing food and livelihood to those who value them. So much for the much vaunted sophistication of western culture!

Banknotes arose as a lighter and easier way for people to carry their symbolic 'gold' around. During my childhood I remember seeing printed on New Zealand banknotes, words to the effect that 'this note can be legally tendered (or exchanged) for X amount of gold', when presented to the appropriate authority. This is the concept underlying the phrase *legal tender*.

You won't find anything like that printed on the money in your wallet, however. Sometime during the 20th century, the idea of potentially having to exchange a dollar note for a specific quantity of gold became impractical to those with economic power, and there is no longer any direct relation between the money that circulates through our society and something physical. *Money* has become a concept, entirely divorced from the material world.

If you have ever used a bank card to complete a purchase, or bought something online, you have participated in treating money as an idea, not a physical item.

These days, stocks and shares, bonds and equities, futures and hedge funds all demonstrate that *money* is simply a concept. A vast quantity of the world's so-called wealth never passes through anyone's hands, but is transferred around the globe via electronic systems that add or subtract zeros to someone's bank account overnight.

The idea that I can somehow rob somebody else by asking the universe for more money continues, partly because it suits the prevailing economic system to keep our belief in scarcity intact, and partly through the deeply ingrained experience of lack in our collective psyche.

Money as Life Force

We started our discussion by considering money as a physical item, and have moved to money as a concept. Let us take a step further and consider money as an energy stream that enables you to have choice.

Freedom of choice is a foundational spiritual principle on which this world operates. Is it then such a far step to consider that money, as an energy that promotes choice, is in fact an expression of the Life Force?

How do you feel about opening up to receive more of the Life Force?

When you step up to make your special contribution to the global jigsaw, you become aligned with your own unique vibration and everything that is attached to it. As you choose to expand more into your own fullness, you inevitably open up to receive a greater degree of Life Force energy coming through you. This will include increased financial resources.

No-One Can Steal the Life Force That Is Yours

The expanding Life Force within you and the blessings that come with it, financial and otherwise, are aligned perfectly to your unique vibration, and your unique contribution. At an energetic level, you cannot receive anyone else's reward, and they cannot receive yours. There is abundant Life Force for everyone.

Western economics is founded on the concept of scarcity, but it has no reality in the spiritual realm, nor in nature. When we look at the world around us, we see that nature operates under principles of balance and abundance, even excess.

Millions of spermatozoa are produced in one ejaculate, although only one is needed to fertilise an egg and create a baby.

A healthy tomato plant in my garden produces more fruit than I can use and enough to share with others. Flowers produce many more seeds than are needed to multiply their life in the next generation. Plants provide not only new seedlings for next year's flowering, but food and shelter for birds and insects, and pleasure to the human eye.

Some years the crop is better than others, sometimes we experience drought or flood that reduces a year's bounty, but over time the effects of sunshine and rain balance each other out when humankind does not interfere.

We live in a planet that has the potential for abundance for all, *when we step into the right relationship with each other and with the planet as a whole*, and choose to live in harmony with spiritual principles.

Choose to Prosper

If you are in a state of struggle right now, know that this is not the divine intention for you. Life does not have to be a struggle. Choose right now to thrive, and actively seek spiritual help to grow your business and your income.

Let go of your ego-mind's idea about how to make money, and how much money you need, and allow your soul-desire to come to the fore to guide you. In making your unique contribution to the world, you open the door to become abundant, including financially, in a way that is aligned with your spiritual purpose.

The Life Force *wants and needs* you to thrive and to prosper. There is a great need for souls who are willing to live life at the highest level possible: spiritually, mentally, emotionally, physically – and financially.

By choosing to thrive in all aspects of life, you make the choice to contribute to the world at a much higher level than if you are struggling. When you choose to be the very best that you can be: the healthiest, the happiest, the most peaceful, the most joyful, the most abundant in all respects, then all of this good energy, including abundant financial resources, can not only bless your own life, but overflow to transform the world around you.

Open up and Ask for More

'Jasmine, stop trying to make do with less – ask for more.' The still, small voice in my head spoke quite clearly as I wandered around the local supermarket, trying to calculate whether or not I had enough money to buy eggs this week. It was 2006, and Robert and I were trying to settle in Reading, near Oxford in England. Despite the fact that we had felt clearly guided to make this attempt, it was not going well.

I was trying to build a business that would not get off the ground, and Robert was looking for work, getting many interviews, but not a single offer of employment. We were living on a Job Seekers allowance for one person, and a credit card that was rapidly approaching its limit. It was a time of great financial anxiety and 'spiritual desert' for us. I had become expert at living on small amounts of money and was proud of myself that on our very tight budget I still managed to save for some special days out.

In contracting down when faced with perceived scarcity, I was behaving in a very human way. But it wasn't a spiritual path; the spiritual invitation is to be open to more.

If you're one of those people who says, 'I just want enough money to get by', I'm here to challenge that desire and that expectation. I believe it is imperative that we open our awareness to expand our financial possibilities, not only for ourselves, but for others. Money gives choice. When we have more than enough for our own needs, we can divert the energy of money to create more possibilities for other people.

In every aspect of life that you allow yourself to be abundantly blessed, you have the potential to become an abundant blessing for your community. *Make the choice to be abundant, so that you can raise the prosperity levels of the world as a whole.*

Share Your Wealth

For too long the energy of money has been associated with greed and corruption. It is time for money to be reclaimed by those of us who work for the forces of good. As an entrepreneur, you have already taken a courageous financial path away from the security of paid employment. The Life Force loves creativity and variety and is primed to support you when you commit to using your gifts for the greater good of the world. Committing to be in alignment with your soul purpose lifts your spiritual effectiveness and global impact up to an even higher level.

As you allow larger quantities of money to flow to you and through you, I encourage you to look for ways to expand the good you do in the world.

Everyone is abundant in some area. Look for ways to give which feel natural to you and bring you joy. Close friends of mine are sharing their abundance by replanting native trees in part of their property, thus allowing the return of bird species whose native habitat has been threatened by the clearing of land for farming. This is a wonderful philanthropic investment in restoring the balance of nature that will benefit many generations to come.

Your interests and circumstances will be unique to you, but look for ways that you can contribute both to nature and to people. In so doing, you take your part in repairing some of the damage done to the fabric of life, by several hundred years of industrial exploitation and human greed.

If it feels appealing to you, I encourage you to set a personal intention of becoming a philanthropist. Philanthropy is financial generosity on a large scale, such as supporting an artist, establishing a School or a Foundation. This will not feel right for every soul. However, all of us have the spiritual privilege and responsibility of sharing abundance.

Main Points of This Chapter
- Our culture is dominated by a mistaken belief in scarcity.
- Nature operates under principles of abundance and balance.
- The Life Force wants and needs you to thrive and prosper.
- Money is an expression of the Life Force that allows choice.
- No-one can steal your Life Force.
- Make the choice to be abundant so you can help others.

What This Means for Your Business
Money is one area which shows up very clearly what signals you are sending into the Quantum Field.

Realise that inner work is business work. *If your financial situation isn't what you want it to be, you absolutely must work on yourself as well as on your business.* Your conscious and unconscious thoughts, beliefs and emotions about the world, your value, and your trust or lack thereof in the Life Force itself, all impact your bottom line even more than your actions.

Keep working on healing your trust and building your relationship with Higher Consciousness. Financial crisis can be a catalyst for accelerated growth and breakthrough. For many people, financial pressure is the point where their ego finally crumbles and they turn to Higher Consciousness for help.

Grow Your Business Action Steps
1. If you haven't already done so, schedule regular time for meditation and prayer into your business calendar. Actively seek the guidance of Higher Consciousness in your business decisions. Ask for help to release any unconscious blocks to financial flow and prosperity.
2. Use the *Financial Abundance* meditation at the end of the chapter on a regular basis.
3. Use the practices of Appreciation and Blessing given in Chapter 15.

Meditation: Opening up to Financial Abundance

Each stage of this meditation is beneficial. Work through it slowly. You can stop part way through and return at any time. Stop at any point you feel negative thoughts or any sort of tension. Invite the healing power of the Life Force to dissolve the source of the tension. Stay at that level of the meditation until you feel light and joyful and trusting. Let yourself become settled and happy at each stage before moving on to the next. Return as often as you need until your thoughts and feelings about money are regularly joyful and positive.

Begin in the usual way, by relaxing and focusing on your breath. Breathe your awareness down into the golden light of love at the centre of the earth.

Imagine that money is floating past you in whatever currency your country uses. Remember that money is transferred electronically around the world all the time. The electronic impulses that manifest as figures in somebody's bank account are travelling through you right now. Let yourself feel open and grateful for the abundant flow of energy that manifests as money.

Imagine that you are in a limitless stream of money constantly flowing around the world. Allow your heart to be open. Let yourself feel grateful, peaceful, joyful and deeply appreciative of the energy of money as it flows continually through the world. If you notice any tension, negative thoughts or judgements about money, however subtle they may be, tap gently on the side of your hand and say quietly, 'I choose to let this go.' Keep tapping and repeating over and over your choice to release negative judgements and beliefs, until you feel peaceful and relaxed.

Once you are relaxed and happy in the limitless stream of money which is flowing through and around you, allow some of it to manifest into your bank account. Then in your imagination create a door on one side of the stream of money for your own use. Which side of the stream is it on? Open the door and go through it. In your imagination, create a special, sacred space for money to fill. Let this space be beautiful, full of sunlight and joy. Fill it with whatever gives your heart pleasure and makes you feel abundant.

Imagine a strong and steady stream of money from the electronic impulses that circle the globe flowing into this space. Allow your room to fill, then hold the connecting door wide open and allow the money to overflow out into the world beyond your room.

Imagine all the people and businesses to whom you give money. See their smiling faces all around you as you allow money to flow through you out into the community. See them blessed and happy, shining with joy and appreciation as they receive what you give them, then turning to go about their lives, allowing money to multiply and create more blessing beyond them. Imagine money flowing from the limitless Life Force through your heart to bless each person and multiply the blessings beyond you.

Imagine yourself as a fount of financial blessing in the world. Let money flow through your heart and your hands. Stay with this awareness for several minutes before finishing your meditation.

Return often to this space that you have created, where money flows effortlessly to you, and through you into the community. By doing this meditation frequently, you reprogramme your unconscious mind to connect money with goodness, and to see the blessing that money brings through you into the community around you. Practise reconnecting to this state of happy generosity and limitless flow whenever you make a financial transaction.

For a recording of the meditation above go to
www.JasmineSampson.com/bookresources

CHAPTER 15
Practise Appreciation and Blessing

It's easy to feel positive when things are going well – it's much harder when your cash flow is drying up, your business is floundering, or you are faced with a crisis of some sort.

In this chapter we look at the skills of Appreciation and Blessing which bring sparkle and sunshine into the most humdrum aspects of daily life.

1. **Appreciation** – is turning up the volume on your enjoyment of 'good stuff'
2. **Blessing** – is strengthening the good in every situation

Appreciation
Radical appreciation is a skill that I am still learning. Whether it is by nature or because of what I learned as a child, my first instinct is always to look for what needs fixing, rather than what I can celebrate right now. As I practise the skill of appreciation on a daily basis, I am finding that everything in my life flows more easily.

Gratitude and appreciation are obviously linked. The subtle difference between them is the degree to which you let yourself feel joy. Gratitude starts in the head and becomes appreciation when you bring those thoughts down and feel them in your heart. Gratitude can feel like something you *ought* to do, while appreciation is something you *genuinely feel*.

This is vitally important because feeling appreciative of your life *as it is right now* will keep you aligned with vibrations that are light and joyful. This in turn will attract into your life circumstances, people and resources to bring even more joy to support you to fulfil your purpose more easily. Appreciation is an enormously valuable skill to develop as part of your daily practice, because it shifts how you feel and therefore shifts the vibrational messages you are sending out into the Quantum Field.

Here are a couple of exercises to 'turn up the volume' of your gratitude and shift you into the joy of appreciation. The first one is designed to be done with a man-made object, the second one with something in nature.

Download an MP3 recording of both these exercises at www.JasmineSampson.com/bookresources

Appreciation Exercise: The Web of Interconnection

Choose an everyday object that you use in your business on a daily basis, perhaps a pen. Hold it in your hands, and think about all the people involved in bringing this object into your life. Here are a few suggestions to stimulate your imagination. Consider:

- Those who sold it to you
- People who brought it from the warehouse to the store
- Those who put all the individual parts together to produce the finished product
- All those involved in the manufacture of each separate part
- Those who invented this particular pen
- The history of pens from the days of feather quills up to the present, and all of the human skill and imagination involved in that development
- Your own ability to write – your teachers and all the ways that you use this basic skill
- All those who contributed to your having the money to make this purchase

By now you will have a good awareness of your interconnectedness to many, many other people far outside your conscious awareness. And all of this through just one tiny object in a small part of your life. You are probably beginning to feel some of the appreciation in your heart already.

Bring your awareness down into your heart area. Focus on that feeling of warmth as you think about all the people that you are connected to via this common everyday object. Spend some time breathing and really focusing on this feeling in your heart centre. Here are some ways you might expand this feeling.

- *Imagine light and love radiating out from you in a network of appreciation that touches everyone connected to this object.*
- *Add colour to this feeling – the first colour you think of or see. Imagine this colour flowing through your body, and radiating in an ever-enlarging spiral out into the world to touch all those whose life and work supports yours.*
- *Allow the warmth of appreciation and the colour you have chosen to fill every part of your body.*
- *Say 'thank you' to all those connected to you via this object.*

Appreciation Exercise: Expanding the Joy

Remember the Head, Heart and Gut Brains I mentioned in Chapter 5? Here is another exercise which will have a beneficial effect on all three intelligence centres as you experience something in nature. I have used a flower to demonstrate the principles, but you can adapt the instructions to whatever you are working with.

Hold the flower in your hands.

- *Start by noticing the feeling of pleasure you have simply looking at this flower.*
- *Use each of your senses in turn to deepen that feeling of pleasure: look in detail at its colour; the formation of its petals; the way it sits on its stem; the arrangement of its stamens …*
- *Inhale its fragrance.*
- *Feel the texture of the petals, the stem, the leaves.*
- *Keep expanding the feeling of pleasure you have in your heart about the flower. Close your eyes and add colour to this feeling.*
- *Keep your eyes closed, and as you breathe in, allow this colour and feeling of pleasure to flow up to your brain. Allow your thoughts to expand your appreciation of this plant.*
- *When you feel ready, with your next out-breath allow the colour and expanded appreciation to flow back down into your heart. Spend some time magnifying and absorbing it further.*

- *When this feels complete, on your next out-breath, swallow and allow the feeling and colour to flow down to your stomach. Circulate the feeling and colour of appreciation and absorb it fully through your Gut Brain. Allow yourself to feel nurtured and satisfied by the pleasure you are taking in this flower. Allow your feeling of appreciation to expand further.*
- *Finally, breathe the colour and feeling back up to your heart and imagine them flowing from the heart throughout your body.*

I find variations of these two exercises enormously helpful in increasing my enjoyment of life. When I think like this, I become aware that I am profoundly connected to an incredible network of people, ideas, things, and nature that expands around the world and back through time.

It helps me feel how my life is supported by many things beyond my own efforts and conscious awareness. It increases my humility and desire to be of service, and increases my trust in the universe.

All of this leads me naturally onto practising the other 'Super Boost' habit of Blessing.

Blessing

One of the most transformative skills you can develop is the habit of Blessing. I was fortunate to learn this while still a child.

When I was a little girl, if I was unhappy at school because one of the other girls was saying or doing unkind things, my wise mother told me to bless the individual in question, every time I thought of her. With the wide open and trusting heart of a child, I did exactly what she said, and every single time these relationships transformed within a very few days. I had invoked the power of Blessing, which connected to the inherent good inside the other child, and dissolved any fear and resentment in my own heart, which would have kept the unkindness in place.

I found it very easy, almost like magic, as a child. The same principle still works for me now, but I have to work much harder to release the judgements which seem to accumulate so easily around my adult ego.

Blessing Strengthens and Transforms

Blessing strengthens what is good and transforms what is not good. When faced with a painful state of affairs or a person who is acting destructively, we can often find it very hard to bless this circumstance, let alone the other person. We mistakenly think that blessing will strengthen the negative aspects of the situation, or imply that we approve or accept what is happening.

The opposite is true. Blessing strengthens the potential good in any situation and calls upon divine power to shift everything else into alignment with it. Blessing is one of the most powerful miracle-producing practices you can do, and I encourage you to incorporate it into your daily toolkit.

It does require effort at first, as your ego-self will come up with all the reasons why you *shouldn't be doing this*, but for those who persevere I promise that you will see a breakthrough. I can't promise when it will happen, as no-one knows how many layers of fear and judgement have to be dissolved first – in you and the other person! As the old advertisement said: 'It won't happen overnight. But it will happen!'

You will probably find health benefits too – as blessing helps to alkalise your body. A few years ago I had a bad attack of mouth ulcers. I discovered that when I used my mouth to bless, the ulcers were less painful and healed more quickly.

Blessing Works in Alignment with Divine Intention

Be aware that blessing is not a rubber stamp for the ego's desires. When it realises just how powerful the habit of blessing can be, the ego-mind can be tempted to use it in manipulative ways, in an attempt to speed up the process of *getting what it wants*. Blessing doesn't work that way.

Blessing works to bring about your soul's true desires in accordance with divine intention. It will always work to bring about the highest good in any situation, which ultimately, of course, is the fastest path to the fulfilment of your heart's true desires. If the results of choosing to bless at first seem different from what you think they should be, persevere anyway. Trust Higher Consciousness to bring about the very best solution, in the very best way, and in the very best time frame for all concerned.

Now isn't that better and easier, than trying to manufacture a solution all by yourself?

How to Bless Everything

You can bless in many ways. Here are a few ideas to get you started:

- The words *Bless you* spoken or thought
- A silent prayer for the highest good for all concerned
- Visualising the person/situation surrounded and filled with love and/or white or golden light
- Sending love and warmth from your heart. This is a natural outflow from the habit of appreciation, as we have already seen

Blessing Your Life and Business

Here are some examples of how you can use the power of blessing for your business and in other aspects of your daily life.

Bless your family and loved ones. Even though my children are now adults with families of their own, each morning as part of my prayer routine I say 'blessing, blessing, blessing' while imagining each family group surrounded and filled with divine light. I give thanks that they are being protected, blessed and guided on their life path.

Bless your food. It will enhance its Life Force and harmonise it for your health. Be aware of all the people who contributed to bringing this food to your table. Allow love to radiate from your heart to bless them and the earth from which all our food comes.

Bless your business plan. A group of business people met weekly during a time of economic depression to support and encourage each other. Each week they would lay hands upon their business plan and together pronounced a prayer of blessing. The businesses concerned not only stayed in operation but grew and prospered through a time when other businesses were closing.

Bless your cash flow, and give thanks for a steady stream of financial resources flowing towards you. Whilst working on this book I had one client who owed me several hundred dollars for an outstanding invoice. I noticed this situation had created tightness in my heart and decided to use the power of blessing to resolve the issue. I imagined him filled with light and asked for a blessing on his prosperity and gave thanks for settlement of his outstanding invoice. The bill was paid within a week.

Bless your clients/customers past, present and future. Keep a notebook with the names of your clients in them. Regularly lay hands upon it and imagine light flowing from your heart and from the universe to bless them and their lives. Include a description of your ideal client or customer in the notebook, and give thanks that the universe is bringing you a steady supply of the people who need your gifts.

Bless yourself, your skills and experience and the gifts you bring to the world. Give thanks for everything in your life which has helped you develop to this point. Ask the universe to continue to bless and prosper you and enable you to serve more people.

Bless your home and workplace and everyone who participates in their creation and maintenance. Many people like to speak to the building itself: give thanks for the vital role it plays in your life and ask for its ongoing support for you and everyone connected to this building. If this seems a strange idea, remember that the entire universe is conscious and responds positively to appreciation and thanks.

Bless your home and surrounding neighbourhood. Take your place as a catalyst of positive change in your area. Imagine light radiating out from your home or business to bless all of those nearby. Allow the light to radiate out from you in a spiral. The more often you use this blessing, the more easily light will flow, and the further it will reach, until you are able to easily bless your entire town or city.

The meditation at the end of this chapter will guide you through this process.

Bless the world around you. In his book, *Secrets of the Lost Mode of Prayer*,[20] Gregg Braden recommends a three-fold blessing anytime we witness suffering of any sort. Blessing those who suffer, blessing what causes the suffering, and blessing those who witness suffering.

Once you start the habit of blessing you will find it a truly transformative exercise that will lift your level of joy and satisfaction, and increase your prosperity and the health of your business in miraculous ways. I am sure you will start thinking of people, things and situations to bless. There are no limits except your own willingness to experiment and be creative with this ancient and powerful spiritual practice.

---

[20] *Secrets of the Lost Mode of Prayer:* p.110-112

Main Points of This Chapter
- Appreciation is gratitude felt in your heart.
- Practicing appreciation for your life as it is right now keeps you aligned with positive vibrations, which will in turn attract more positive things to appreciate.
- The practice of blessing strengthens what is good and transforms what is not good in any situation.
- Blessing can be done in many ways.
- Both *Blessing* and *Appreciation* are powerful practices that will increase your personal joy and attract improved circumstances in every part of your life.

What This Means for Your Business
I think of *Blessing* and *Appreciation* as being rather like super-boost fertiliser that you put on the garden. Choosing to incorporate these spiritual tools into your business life gives you direct access to the creative power of the universe. They are spiritual superpowers and reap exponential rewards the longer they are used.

At the level of the Quantum Field these practices spread your light to the universe in an unparalleled way – which is a form of 'invisible marketing' that will attract the right clients, resources and opportunities to you without you having to spend a penny! Why do things the slow, hard way when you could get there quicker, easier and with a much bigger positive impact?

Grow Your Business Action Steps
1. Schedule time daily in your calendar to practise the skills of *Appreciation* and *Blessing* for your business.
2. Keep a record in your journal of what you have blessed and the results you are getting as you extend this practice. It will help build your trust and faith. A real estate agent I know blessed her list of potential vendors for just 2 days before being called with a new listing.
3. Stay open-hearted as you pay your bills. Rather than feeling constrained from a belief that you have limited means, allow yourself to see paying your bills as a way of *paying it forward* into the community. As you pay each bill imagine the people and situations that it represents. Let yourself feel grateful for each one, and send a blessing to them as you make payment.

A Blessing Meditation

Begin your meditation in the usual way: sitting or lying with your back straight and your weight evenly distributed. Let your hands lie open in your lap and take several deep calming breaths in through your nose, and out through your mouth, letting your whole body relax more and more on every out-breath.

Breathe your awareness down into the earth and into your sacred space within the golden light of love.

Imagine a beautiful white light shining brightly in your heart centre. Gently focus your attention on it. As you continue to breathe gently and steadily, this light becomes brighter and brighter, until it fills your entire body and radiates out to fill the entire space around you.

Keep your awareness on the centre of the light, as you let yourself feel more and more calm, and relaxed and joyful. Rest for as long as you wish in this beautiful healing frequency. If there are any particular concerns or questions that you have, speak them quietly into the light. Let go and trust that the answer will come in the perfect way at the perfect time. Stay with your own questions and concerns until you are feeling centred and happy, and ready to radiate this blessing to others.

Imagine this beautiful light beginning to spin gently clockwise in a circle all around you. As you stay focused on the movement, the light grows bigger and stronger and begins to spiral out in an ever-expanding circle. It extends to fill your body, and the space around you. It continues to expand into the building you are in, and beyond it into the neighbourhood. Focus on remaining relaxed, calm and open, as you allow the energy of the light to expand effortlessly in every direction around you.

From this relaxed and open state, gently bring to mind your family, your loved ones and anyone else that you wish to bless today. Each person will find their own comfortable distance within the orbit of the light. Imagine the light flowing effortlessly around through and upon them, filling them with light and joy, peace and harmony. You may wish to speak some words or prayers of blessing. You can do this silently or aloud.

Rest in this ever expanding circle of light for as long as you wish. Imagine light flowing out from you in every direction. Trust the intelligence of the light to go where it is needed and to touch whoever it wants to touch. Let yourself feel light and peaceful and happy.

When you are ready to finish your meditation, say 'thank you' *to the healing intelligence of the light. Imagine it shrinking down back inside your body until it is like a candle flame, glowing gently in your heart. Breathe your awareness back up into your body. Stretch gently, feeling your feet on the floor and reconnecting fully with your body before you open your eyes.*

Go to www.JasmineSampson.com/bookresources for resources and an MP3 versions of this meditation.

CHAPTER 16
An Invitation to the Adventure of Your Lifetime

The principles and practices outlined in this book guide you to partner with the Life Force to grow your business and make your unique and essential contribution to the world.

By applying these principles, you have the opportunity to fulfil your greatest potential. Through your connection to the Quantum Field, they also enable you to help change human consciousness and participate in creating a new experience for the planet as a whole. It is the adventure of a lifetime.

Know that you are not alone in your endeavour. The Life Force is alert and attentive to your heart's desires and the creative force of the entire universe is supporting your desire to be and to do more than you have ever known.

Learning to Surf

The cycles of night and day, moon and tides, seasons and our personal energy levels all reflect the fact that we are part of an energetic system that is constantly moving and changing. Rather than fighting against the constant pull of change, by adopting the practices in this book you will learn to relax and go with the flow of change, so that you become like a surfer riding the waves.

As you become more securely grounded in your being as an essential expression of the Life Force, it will become much easier to allow things around you to move and change. I view this process as *resting on the unchanging bedrock of Spirit*. It is like being connected to the deep water of the ocean bed, which remains calm and undisturbed by storms on the surface.

Stages on the Journey

In Part I we looked at how to grow your relationship with the universe itself. We began with a quick tour of the findings of quantum research to discover that everything in our material world arises out of a Quantum Field of underlying consciousness, and that our predominant emotions, thoughts and words all communicate with this field to play a primary role in our experience of daily life. You realised that your conscious and unconscious emotions have a deciding part to play in the success of your business.

Chapter 2 took us into the nature and *The Power of Love* as the essence of the Life Force that creates and sustains the cosmos, and introduced the idea that committing to be a channel for love enables your life and business to fulfil their highest possibility.

In Chapters 3, *Meditate Daily*, and 4, *Pray*, we explored the practices of meditation and prayer which strengthen your connection to the still calm place of loving wisdom that is inside you, and discovered how scheduling a daily time of silence is an essential step for business success.

Chapter 5 took us into the difference between belief and faith, and discussed how we are all affected by humanity's lack of *Trust in the Universe*. You discovered why investing time and effort into healing your own trust in the Life Force would revolutionise every aspect of your life.

In Chapter 6 I used the experience of my father to illustrate the vital importance of your doing what you are designed to do, and took a look at your life purpose in the context of seven soul themes. We finished the chapter with a guided meditation to help you experience your own unique place in the *Global Jigsaw*.

We looked in some detail at the subject of *Guidance* in Chapter 7, before moving on to explore conscious co-creation with the Life Force in *Harness the Power of Intention* in Chapter 8. Both these chapters gave ways to connect to Higher Consciousness as a deliberate strategy to grow your business.

We finished Part I by turning our attention to the ancient concept of *Shalom* and discovered that it embraces many intertwined concepts, including health, peace, harmony, safety, and prosperity. We realised that committing to live from spiritual principles positions you to receive far more from life than simply cash in exchange for time and services rendered.

Having thoroughly explored your relationship with the universe, we now turned our attention to other key relationships in your life:

Part II gave you ways to grow your relationship with yourself by *Embracing your Uniqueness* and *Practising Forgiveness*.

Part III explored the subtle difference between judgement and discernment and taught you how to *Let go of Judgement* and *Use the Technology of Love* to transform your relationships with other people.

Finally in Part IV we turned our attention to your relationship with the world around you: first with a chapter encouraging you to *Ask for More Money* as an expression of the Life Force in Chapter 14, and then Chapter 15 finished off the section with the transformative practices of *Appreciation and Blessing*.

What Now?

You have a choice. You could put this book aside and say, '*That was interesting*', and continue life and business as before.

Alternatively, you could say "*Yes*" to the bigger possibility for your life and business, and open up to the adventure of a lifetime by investing 15 minutes a day and one hour a week to implement the practices you have learned here.

The choice is yours.

Let's Stay in Touch

If you're implementing even one tiny part of what I have suggested here, please stay in touch. If you haven't already connected with me online, please do so by claiming your free resources at www.JasmineSampson.com/bookresources. You will receive regular updates and tips from me, and be kept informed of special training, new releases and special 'reader-only' offers.

I would love to hear your questions and experiences as you put into practice what you have learned in this book. Just reply to one of my emails or use the contact form on my website *www.JasmineSampson.com*

What you do actually *matters*. In reading this book and applying the principles you learn here, you are part of a steadily growing group of exceptional people who are not content with the status quo, and are stepping up to maximise their potential and fill their unique place in the world.

Thank you for taking time to purchase and read this book and to apply the principles you have learned here. Most of all *thank you* for being you and bringing your unique talents and experience to help us all evolve and grow.

There is nothing more for me to say except that –

I believe in YOU.
Your life makes a difference.
The world NEEDS you and your gifts.

BIBLIOGRAPHY

Braden, Gregg. *The Divine Matrix: Bridging time, space, miracles, and belief.* New York: Hay House, 2008.

– *Secrets of the Lost Mode of Prayer: The hidden power of beauty, blessings, wisdom, and hurt.* New York: Hay House, 2006.

Brinkley, Dannion, and Kathryn Brinkley. *Secrets of the Light: The incredible true story of one man's near-death experiences and the lessons he received from the other side.* London: Piatkus, 2009.

Brueggemann, Walter. 'The Costly Loss of Lament.' *JSOT* 6, 57–71, 1986.

Cortens, Theolyn. *Working with Your Guardian Angel: An inspirational 12-week programme for finding your life's purpose.* London: Piatkus, 2005.

Dyer, Wayne. *The Power of Intention: Learning to co-create your world your way.* Australia: Griffin Press, 2004.

– *There's a Spiritual Solution to Every Problem.* Australia: HarperCollins, 2001.

Edwards, Glyn, and Santoshan. *Unleash Your Spiritual Power and Grow: Reflect - and learn to trust the power within.* Sydney: Quantum, 2007.

Foundation for Inner Peace. *A Course in Miracles.* Authorised by Dr. Helen Schucman, Scribe. Tiburon, CA, 1975, 1985.

Frankl, Viktor E. *Man's Search for Meaning: An introduction to logotherapy.* First published 1946 (in German). New York: Beacon, 1959.

Goswami, Dr. Amit. *God is Not Dead: What quantum physics tells us about our origins and how we should live.* Charlottesville, VA: Hampton Roads, 2008.

Hawker, Paul. *Soul Survivor: A spiritual quest through 40 days in the wilderness.* Oxford: Lion Books, 2001.

Hicks, Esther, and Jerry Hicks. *The Amazing Power of Deliberate Intent: Living the art of allowing.* Carlsbad CA: Hay House, 2006

Jampolsky, Gerald G. *Teach Only Love: The twelve principles of attitudinal healing.* New York: Bantam, 1981.

– *Love is Letting Go of Fear.* Berkley CA: Celestial Arts, 1979.

Nelson, Martia. *Coming Home: The return to true self.* Sebastopol CA: Martia Nelson, 2011.

Oka, Marvin, and Grant Soosalu. *mBraining: Using your multiple brains to do cool stuff.* Victoria Australia: mBit International Pty Ltd, 2012.

Ponder, Catherine. *Dynamic Laws of Prayer.* Camarillo, CA: DeVorss & Co, 1987.

– *The Prospering Power of Love.* Revised edition. Marina Del Rey, CA: DeVorss & Co, 2006.

Williamson, Marianne. *A Return To Love: Reflections on the principles of a course in miracles.* New York: HarperCollins, 1992.

ACKNOWLEDGMENTS

A book is a collaborative venture and many people are owed thanks. Here are some of the most obvious.

First my parents, Val and Selwyn Sampson. Mum, you taught me to forgive and to bless and that there is a spiritual power available to help me in everyday life. And Dad, because the restrictions you experienced have made me aware of my own choices and helped shape my values. Thank you for the gift of life and for nurturing my childhood faith.

My sons – Matthew, Nicholas and Simon –who were the catalyst of my awakening to consciousness, and their father Harry Poole, who in life supported my growth and whose death catapulted me into new possibilities.

My clients who have helped me refine what I offer and propelled my growth in ways you will never know. Jenny, Judy, and Bernadette of ISOUL, for your constant encouragement and support. Bernie and Graham, for reading early drafts of this material and offering useful feedback. Annemarie, for being another early reader, and especially for fabulous afternoon teas, enthusiastic encouragement and unwavering friendship.

Sarah, for your prayer support, nurturing friendship and being the first person to read and edit the completed text. Elizabeth Thuan, who kept encouraging me to write, and patiently waited for a text to edit before putting her professional skills to work so effectively. You both helped to shape a conglomeration of ideas and processes into the book it is today.

Janet Beckers, who has offered a wealth of advice about how to make this material available to those who need it, and Linda Diggle and everyone at Book Boffin who have made the process of publishing such a delight.

And most of all to my beloved Robert, who keeps encouraging me to become my best self – and who believed in this book long before it began to be written. Sharing my life with you is an ongoing adventure. Thank you.

www.ingramcontent.com/pod-product-compliance
Lightning Source LLC
Chambersburg PA
CBHW071403290426
44108CB00014B/1665